Tony 1C

ABOUT THE AUTHORS

Tony O'Reilly is a former An Post branch manager originally from Carlow. After losing everything to a gambling addiction he resolved to put his experiences to good use and today he is a fully qualified counsellor dedicated to raising awareness of gambling addiction. If you wish to get in touch with him, you can find him on LinkedIn (Tony O'Reilly MACI).

Declan Lynch is an author and columnist with the *Sunday Independent*. A prominent commentator on matters of culture, sport and politics, he is also the author of ten books, including *Days of Heaven*, *John Giles: A Football Man* and *The Ponzi Man*.

TONY 10

The astonishing story of the postman who
gambled €10,000,000 . . . and lost it all

**Declan Lynch
&
Tony O'Reilly**

Gill Books

Gill Books
Hume Avenue
Park West
Dublin 12
www.gillbooks.ie

Gill Books is an imprint of M.H. Gill and Co.

978 07171 7970 1

Designed by Carole Lynch
Print origination by O'K Graphic Design, Dublin
Edited by Rachel Pierce
Proofread by Neil Burkey

Printed by CPI Group (UK) Ltd, Croydon CRO 4YY
This book is typeset in 13.5/17 pt Minion.

The paper used in this book comes from the wood pulp of managed forests. For every tree felled, at least one tree is planted, thereby renewing natural resources.

A CIP catalogue record for this book is available from the British Library.

5 4 3 2

PROLOGUE

I t was a beautiful thing.

According to Dennis Bergkamp, the Dutch footballer who did this beautiful thing, 'it's like your life has led up to this moment ... you never play the perfect game, but the moment itself was, I think, perfect.'

This perfect moment took place in the second last minute of Holland's World Cup quarter-final against Argentina in Marseille on 4 July 1998. Bergkamp was running hard towards the end-line, chasing a long pass from Frank de Boer into the Argentina penalty area. He gained complete control of the ball with his first touch, which was quite a thing in itself, but which on this day was the first of three sublime movements made into one. The second touch put the Argentina defender Ayala out of the picture, the third was a flick past the goalkeeper with the outside of Bergkamp's right foot into the top left-hand corner of the net – and it was a beautiful, beautiful thing.

Some commentators say it is the physical elegance of Bergkamp that lends an extra dimension to his most famous goals, but it is also the quickness of his mind. It is the fact that in order to accomplish this, he had to have worked it all out instantly, instinctively: seeing the long pass from de Boer coming in his direction, deciding that the only successful outcome would have to involve this three-point manoeuvre, with the most extreme degree of difficulty. Then he executes it, just as he had imagined it, and he is running towards the corner flag, celebrating, until he is taken down by his orangeshirted team-mates, who raise their arms and roar with delirium as Bergkamp lies there under the perfect blue sky of Marseille, knowing that he has put his country into the semi-final of the World Cup.

The Dutch all over the world were feeling this ecstasy, not just because of the victory but because Bergkamp had done something so outrageously brilliant. That goal had immediately ascended to a high place in the illustrious history of the Dutch game. But this was not just a glorious day for the people of Holland. In Ireland, in the town of Carlow, in a pub called Scraggs Alley, there was a man working behind the bar who was feeling a similar ecstasy. He celebrated as he watched that beautiful moment, and he would continue to celebrate for the rest of the day and all through the evening. He celebrated like he had never known that such elation was possible. Like his whole life had led up to this moment.

◆ ◆ ◆

On the morning of 4 July 1998, Tony O'Reilly was in Scraggs Alley, standing behind the bar, chatting to a customer, Brendan, about the game and the day ahead. He was looking forward to all of it. He was due to go to a wedding reception later that night with his girlfriend. He had been at work since 9.30 a.m., organising the stock and the ice and giving the place an extra polish. He was looking forward to the big fry-up that he and his colleagues would enjoy at lunchtime, as they did every Saturday, about six of them sitting down together in the main lounge to eat a big Irish breakfast.

Tony had been working in Scraggs for a few years, but since February 1998 he was also working as a part-time postman, doing about twenty hours a week, which he fit around his bar shifts. Among the few worries he had in life, perhaps the main one was that all this working might interfere with his soccer, which he was taking seriously – he played centre-forward with a leading local team called Stretford United. For a Liverpool fan the name of the team was an obvious embarrassment. Indeed, one of Tony's team-mates, John, who was also a Liverpool fan, used to cover the club crest with black insulating tape to make himself feel better about it. The team had been successful in the local cup competitions, but when it came to the league they were regarded as Jimmy White-type figures – forever coming second when they should have won it.

These were the issues that preoccupied the mind of this twenty-four-year-old on a sunny day in July, during the World Cup. He remembers it clearly as a sunny day, maybe even as sunny in the Irish southeast as it was in Marseille. Scraggs would be a bit busier than usual due to the match in the afternoon and the other one later in the evening, Croatia v Germany. The back bar would be open tonight, with Matt the DJ playing the music.

Maybe it was the promise of all the sport to come, or the wedding, or maybe it was just the good weather and the good vibes, but as Tony spoke to Brendan at the bar that morning, he decided to do something he had never done before. He decided to place a bet. They had talked about the football for a while, then Brendan got up to leave the pub and go down to the Paddy Power office. Tony was due to take his break, so he said, 'Sure, I'll go down with you.'

Just to have an interest. That was the thought in his head as he decided to go and put a few quid on the game. Just to have an interest.

He had reached the age of twenty-four without ever placing a bet, or even entering the premises of a bookmaker. When he did so on this day, he was not greatly excited by what he found there. There were a few televisions, but not the big bank of screens you would find today in any betting office. It was all relatively primitive, with prices displayed on sheets of paper, and generally not much to persuade the visitor to spend any great amount of time there.

Tony saw that Patrick Kluivert was 6/1 to score the first goal of the game. For most Irish football people, Kluivert had been a significant presence since the night, in 1995, when he had led Holland's destruction of the Republic of Ireland in a European Championship play-off at Anfield. Kluivert had arrived that night as a young player of immense promise. Unfortunately for Ireland, his emergence ended the happiest period of our football lives, the years from 1986 to 1995, which became known as the Charlton era.

We knew how good Kluivert was. Too good for us, certainly.

Tony read the odds and with the clarity of thought of a man who had never done this before, and who has no intention of doing it again, he decided to have a punt. He put IR£1 on Kluivert at 6/1 to score the first goal.

Brendan had also seen a bet that he liked. He was looking at Holland to beat Argentina 2–1. With the pure enthusiasm of men who don't really care all that much anyway, they decided to merge the two propositions. They each ended up having IR£1 on Kluivert to score the first goal of the game and Holland to win 2–1, at the wondrous odds of 45/1.

Kluivert scoring the first goal would not be enough. Holland winning 2–1 would not be enough. They needed both of these things to happen, and though Tony was new to this, he knew that the odds accurately reflected their chances of success, which were virtually zero.

But it was only a pound. And it meant he would have an interest.

He even needed help in filling out the betting slip, a scene which seemed to confirm the underlying absurdity of the notion that you can be sitting there in Carlow thinking you can predict with such ludicrous precision the outcome of a great event, with an infinite number of imponderables, taking place that afternoon in the South of France.

And it was a great event, a game with moments of high quality. Acting on the advice of Eamon Dunphy on his *The Last Word* radio programme, some had invested in Argentina at the start of the tournament, at odds of 14/1, which was looking pretty damn good now that they were in the quarter-final, this team of Diego Simeone, Javier Zanetti, Ariel Ortega, Juan Sebastián Verón, Hernán Crespo and Gabriel Batistuta.

But Holland had Edwin van der Sar, Frank de Boer, Edgar Davids, Marc Overmars, Patrick Kluivert and Dennis Bergkamp.

And they had Tony O'Reilly's money too, bringing with it the luck of the punter who has never done this before, and who may never do it again, declaring that Patrick Kluivert will score the first goal and Holland will win 2–1, standing behind the bar of Scraggs Alley as the match kicks off at 3.30, wanting this to happen for him.

Kluivert scored the first goal, after twelve minutes.

Tony was lifted by this, but he knew enough about football to know that a thousand things could happen in the remaining seventy-eight minutes to wreck his hopes. They last for such a long time, football matches.

Five minutes later, Argentina equalised. The striker, Claudio López, in an act of almost disgraceful audacity, stuck it through the legs of Edwin van der Sar when he had easier options. It was 1–1. Kluivert had scored first. It was certainly not out of the question that Holland could win 2–1. Now Tony was seriously involved.

Until this moment it had been no big deal. From this moment until the end of the game, it all escalated for him. The adrenaline started racing through him. That equaliser by Claudio López had given him a feeling almost like the euphoria he got from scoring a goal for his own team, that same sense of being utterly alive, a feeling he hadn't thought was available to him anywhere else in this world. And that was just the start of it.

For the next seventy minutes he was mesmerised by the possibilities and the permutations racing through his head, praying for Argentina not to score, praying for Holland to get one more goal, but not two. It looked like it was going to be taken away from him after about seventy minutes when the Dutch defender Numan was sent off for a foul on Simeone, who went spinning across the turf in a kind of ecstasy of agony. It looked particularly doubtful when both Ortega and Batistuta hit the post for Argentina. And in the last few minutes it seemed that the bet was about to go down when Ortega went flying, claiming what seemed like a stonewall penalty.

Somehow the referee saw what the replays later revealed, that Ortega had executed a truly convincing dive. And perhaps in his frustration that he had been thwarted in this dark enterprise, Ortega got into a confrontation with the keeper, van der Sar, which the referee interpreted as a head-butt. He sent off the Argentinian for that and for the dive, making it ten against ten for the last few minutes and for the extra time that seemed sure to follow.

For Tony O'Reilly, it had turned around again, it was an even contest once more. But it was still maddeningly uncertain – he knew just enough about the betting game to know that the 2–1 scoreline had to happen within the ninety minutes, that the score after extra time wouldn't count.

He was so riveted by it now, it didn't seem to matter anymore that it was only a pound – it felt like he stood to lose a lot more than that.

Still the bet was alive, so much had gone right that could have gone wrong. Still, for a few more minutes, there was hope.

Then Bergkamp did what Bergkamp did.

◆ ◆ ◆

Tony O'Reilly celebrated in Scraggs Alley with a few drinks, reminiscing about the glories of the day, the wonder of turning a quid into 45 quid, which at the time was maybe half a week's wages. The wonder of it all.

He reflected on the fact that there had been an unwitting major contribution from a Spanish referee who, in the previous round, had inexplicably declined to send off Bergkamp when he had, equally inexplicably, stamped on the Yugoslavia player Siniša Mihajlović. So Bergkamp shouldn't have been playing at all in Marseille. It was just another of the lucky breaks that had enabled Tony to win the bet, as if some force had decreed that this should happen, and nothing was going to prevent it.

By the time he got to the wedding that evening, Tony was quite exhausted by the beer and the adrenaline, but in the deepest part of his being he was still elated. He had seen something that day, and felt something, that was better than anything else he had seen or felt in his life. The man who had never been in a betting office until this day, who had never had much interest in gambling, had fallen instantly in love with it.

And when eventually he fell into his bed that night, he lay there thinking about what seemed to him the greatest thing of all: how easy it had been.

PART ONE

CHAPTER 1

Tony O'Reilly is from Carlow, and he was formed by its unassuming nature. There is something understated about Carlow.

The second smallest county in Ireland does not draw attention to itself – even the fact that it is the second smallest, rather than the smallest, seems to suggest some underlying desire not to be noticed. There is no strong Carlow accent, you never hear Carlow people being impersonated like those of Cork or Cavan or Donegal. Sitting next to the counties of Wicklow, Wexford, Kildare, Laois and Kilkenny, it is the modest neighbour.

In towns such as Borris or Bagenalstown there are shades of a faded grandeur and yet these places, just like Hacketstown or Tullow, give the impression that they are not exactly desperately seeking your approval. There has been a large Regional College in Carlow since 1970, but you will rarely hear Carlow being described as a 'lively student town'. In fact, it's hard to even say what kind of town it is. This vagueness of identity is matched by the question mark over whether Carlow is in the south-east or in the midlands, or perhaps both. Yet it is quite attractive, this vagueness, this lack of posturing; it allows you to make up your own mind about the place.

It is unassuming too about its status as the town with the first large sugar factory in Ireland, founded in 1926, a result of a policy by the new State to encourage the growth of native industries with the result that generations of schoolchildren had the names of the four Irish sugar factories drilled into them – Carlow, Mallow, Thurles, Tuam.

Not only was the national reputation of Carlow based on the making of sugar, it dominated the atmosphere of the town due to the powerful aroma which would emerge from the factory, the smell of the beet being processed which some regarded as foul, but which was also fondly regarded for all it was bringing to the town – or is it only a town? With a population of around 18,000, Carlow is by some measurements a town, and by others a city, neither one nor the other. Which, again, is something about which Carlow people seem relaxed.

Tony O'Reilly's father, Tony Senior, had worked for Irish Sugar since 1961, specifically for Armer Salmon, which was the trading name of the agricultural engineering section of the company. When Tony Junior was seventeen, he was offered the chance to do an interview for an apprenticeship as an electrician with Armer Salmon. He knew it was a chance to get a foothold on a decent career, and he told his father that he'd go to the interview. But he didn't go to it.

His father let him know that he was very annoyed by this, and indeed his father's annoyance was understandable. But deep down Tony's wasn't really bothered that he had adopted such a casual approach to this opportunity. What of it? And yet years later he would start to see a deeper significance in this refusal to step up and give it a chance. Looking back, he wondered if this incident had left him with a kind of a guilt complex, planting in him the need for affirmation. He uses words like *wayward, carefree, bulletproof* to describe his sense of estrangement from the forces of life in general and his attitude to this chance in particular. He thought then that he would have other chances that were more to his liking.

And as it turned out, it may not have been an entirely wrong decision. In the early 1990s when Tony was up for that interview, a job in the sugar factory may have seemed like a secure enough position, yet in 2007, after eighty years as a great institution in Carlow it was closed with the loss of 190 full-time and 130 seasonal jobs.

If he had gone for the job at the age of seventeen, and stayed there until it was shut down, moving up the grades, he would have been in his early thirties when he was given his redundancy, probably with commitments that would now be hard to fulfil.

But that's not how it looked in 1991, when Tony O'Reilly got a chance in life that most young men of his age in Carlow would have been delighted to accept, and walked away from it like he was turning down a shift in the local McDonald's.

It wasn't that he was unaware of the need to make a living, far from it. In term time, his parents hosted students from Carlow Regional in their home, to earn a bit of extra cash. It was an arrangement that left Tony with a sense of not having his own space. It made the spare room, which was 'his', the place where he kept his large collection of CDs, seem like a holy place. He knew he wanted proper space of his own, and he was in no doubt that even a small amount of money could make a big difference.

But still he didn't go to the interview at the sugar factory.

Whatever impulses blinded him to this opportunity, oddly enough it probably wasn't a lack of ambition. He recalls his teenage years as being a strange mix of breezing through life and then being quite focused, of drifting along on the outside of things and then connecting with something that really engaged him.

He got into stamp collecting for a while – something about the neatness and orderliness of the process appealed to him.

He was always eager to work for what he wanted, too. When
he was thirteen he was a partner in a business. In a scene that
would normally feature in the story of some tycoon explaining
how he got started, Tony and his friend, Eddie O'Sullivan, set
up a gardening business. They bought a lawn-mower and they
cut grass and hedges. They called themselves Edmow. They
even had business cards printed to promote their enterprise.
Tony recently found one of the business cards, the last remnant
of the little empire that was Edmow. It made him remember
how the two of them had cycled down to Quinnsworth to get
the cards done in a machine outside the supermarket.

Not many thirteen-year-olds in Carlow, or anywhere else,
had their own business cards. It wasn't his only revenue
stream either. When the gardening was slow, he did a lot of
babysitting work, not quite on an industrial scale, but enough
that it could justifiably be called a business too.

He did not have the confident manner of the young
businessman, however. When he was eight years old he'd
struggled for a while with a stammer, and though he had
overcome that, he was still guarded in his dealings with people.
His friend Eddie was the extrovert, and at times Tony would
feel like a loner even within this partnership. Though his
ideas for making money were grown-up, he looked younger
than he was. That strange mix again – young and old, drifter
and focused, ambitious and shy.

He did like the feeling of having his own few pounds in
his pocket, though, which was the driving force behind his
schemes. And he liked the feeling of spending it more than
the feeling of saving it. He would spend it not just on CDs
and clothes, the usual stuff that young men might indulge in,
but on quality goods in general. He bought the best sound
equipment, for example, to satisfy not just his need to have
music at the centre of his life but also a kind of a perfectionist

streak. There was an obsessive quality to this, which emerged later, in his early teens, with the acquisition of an Amstrad CPC 464, which his father bought for the family.

The Amstrad gave young Tony access to games that would consume him for hours. In particular, he played a fruit-machine game in this compulsive fashion, so absorbed in it that he can still recall the sound of the cassette going into the Amstrad, declaring the start of another session on the green screen. More than thirty years later that sound is still with him, as is the noise it made when the three 7's came up on the fruit-machine. He also remembers vividly the feeling he got when he had a near miss, and the urge to complete a three-in-a-row. Effectively, it was his first gambling experience, albeit one that involved no money.

He knew from early on that he would need some sort of decent cash-flow, if only to pay for his tastes in home entertainment, but he didn't believe much success in that line could come from applying himself to school work. *Could do better* – these words or variations on the theme were used often in school reports. *A bit of a dreamer.*

Though his dreams had also helped to create Edmow, he did not have any use for them in school or even on the football field. He had been a promising footballer until he reached the under-14s, and then he stopped playing altogether until eventually he came back to it at nineteen.

He drifted out of contention for the Leaving Certificate by deciding, at the last minute, that he would take mostly Pass papers. He went for the Honours paper in English, but otherwise took the easier options across the board. His motives were mainly negative ones, to do with lack of belief in his academic ability, the thought of the financial stress on the family of his going to university, and his calculation of what he might need to scrape into Carlow Regional. He would even fall asleep during the Accounting exam, after working a late night as a 'floor boy' in the Seven Oaks Hotel, in the nightclub of which, Mimes, a young Ray D'Arcy could be found DJ-ing on Friday nights.

When his Leaving Cert results came through, they were mediocre, apart from one interesting feature. He achieved a B in Honours English. It has always been difficult to get a B or higher in Honours English. It shows promise, a definite talent for the subject. Tony figures it was the essay question that did it for him: write an essay with the title 'The Power of the Imagination'.

He took a chance with it and set off on a track that most other students would probably have found a bit risky. He cited pornography as an example of the dark power of the imagination, contrasting it with the more creative side, which he illustrated with a description of the child who is given a big box of toys, and ends up playing with the box.

Perhaps the examiner was just grateful to be reading an essay about something other than the beauty of Nature and the urge of the Poet to give expression to it. Whatever it was, it was enough to gain him an impressive result.

He was delighted with his grade, but it did have the slight downside of making him wonder if he should have taken a more substantial risk by going for Honours papers in the other subjects. He wondered if he should just have worked harder, instead of looking for the easy way through. It wasn't that he was expecting anything from his Leaving Cert. or himself – he was going no further than Carlow Regional no matter what. But it was another instance of this pattern whereby a sense of aimlessness and apathy would be blown away by some kind of success, once his energies were properly engaged. It gave him an uncomfortable feeling that he might be good at something, he just didn't know what it was.

CHAPTER 2

There is usually a period in people's lives they look back on most fondly, a time, often in their late teens and early twenties, when they seemed to have very little to bother them and all the time in the world to enjoy that happy state. This is how it is with Tony O'Reilly.

He had indeed managed enough points in the Leaving to scrape into Carlow Regional, and he spent an academic year there, nominally studying Electrical Engineering. All the while, though, he wanted to be out in the world with a few pounds in his pocket – deep down, ever since he was thirteen and running his own businesses, that's what he'd wanted.

In the end, he got what he wanted. After one year of a two-year course he left the Regional in 1992 with no qualification, but now he was out there, working for a while in a petrol station and then as a waiter in a restaurant above Scraggs, a place called the Back Door. When that closed down he moved to Portlaoise, moved away from home for the first time, and cooked burgers and kebabs in a diner called Fat Bob's. He will tell you that he cooked a mean kebab. He had never been much into drinking, but he spent a lot of time playing snooker at a club in Graiguecullen.

In late 1993 the offer of a full-time job in Scraggs brought him back to Carlow, maybe to the best place in Carlow for any young person at that time. It was not just a lucky break in itself to get a job there, it was a position that wouldn't have existed at all if some existing employees hadn't been let go, their misfortune becoming Tony's good fortune. Thus began what was to become probably the happiest period in his life.

To get a sense of what a major operation Scraggs was, on Tony's first night working behind the bar there was a Happy Hour during which pints of Budweiser were going for a pound. In that hour they sold 800 pints. On the following night it was Harp Lager going cheap, and 600 pints were sold in the hour. It was the busiest bar in town, and also the biggest venue. Artists such as the Saw Doctors, The Stunning, Don Baker and Aslan all came to play the room upstairs. There was also an excellent local band called Zak Same and the Similars and they played Stevie Wonder covers, funky music in general, and a version of 'Kung Fu Fighting' that always got Tony out on the dancefloor, no more the introverted teenager.

He recalls this local sense that if you got a job in Scraggs, you had made it. There were roughly forty people in all employed there, as bar staff, floor staff, bouncers, cleaners, in the cellar and in the office. They were not just colleagues, they were friends. Tony had a feeling that they were a kind of family – and he thrived on this sense of belonging. Scraggs sponsored his football team, Stretford United, so there were great days and nights when they'd win a cup final and bring the trophy back to the bar to celebrate. He was forming friendships that would last until the present day, with Paul, PJ, 'Wully', Ciaran, Paddy, Andy, 'Uncle Muk'.

Niall Byrne was working the floor at that time, but he would move up and work alongside Tony when they became shift managers. A slightly built but a very large character in Tony's life, Niall would become the sort of friend who, in the fullness of time, Tony found he could trust completely. He was smart and funny and unwaveringly loyal. If one of them needed to borrow money, the other would just give it to him, no questions asked, a courtesy that might even involve the handing over of a credit or debit card until such time as it could be handed back again, again no questions asked. On nights when they were 'blackguarding', as Tony calls it, Niall might use Tony's name, or vice versa, when phoning from the pub for a Chinese takeaway, so that the other would get the blame if they weren't in a position to collect the food. Or one of them would order a large round of drinks in the other's name without the other's knowledge, waiting to observe the reaction.

Eventually they would assume more responsibilities, and in fact Niall would eventually become the manager of Scraggs, but in these early days it was all about the blackguarding.

When he wasn't free to perform variations of 'Kung Fu Fighting' on the dancefloor upstairs, Tony was in the downstairs bar, playing pool or just listening to the jukebox. He had always come to Scraggs for the music anyway, for the CDs behind the counter. He remembers hearing a lot of The Cure and Pink Floyd and Nirvana's *Unplugged* and Pearl Jam's *10* around that time. On the jukebox Gwen Stefani's 'Don't Speak' saw a lot of action, and 'Ace of Spades' by Motörhead would be roaring at all hours.

There were days of chaos when the students from the Regional arrived into Scraggs in large numbers on the day of a big college football match. Usually on these occasions the students were given a keg of beer by way of sponsorship, and issued tickets with which they could redeem their share of the keg. It might involve up to ninety tickets being handed out to them, but if somehow they failed to complete the course, Tony and his associates were always there to complete it for them.

Sometimes they'd end up drinking the students' beer and their own beer in Scraggs, listening to the jukebox and shooting pool and playing pontoon and Texas Hold 'Em and generally acting the maggot and having a wonderful time. On these nights, long before the smoking ban, the atmosphere would be very, very smoky. There was an open fire with a big brown leather chair beside it, which was always in demand. It was called 'the comfy chair', too comfy in fact one Christmas for a late-night drinker who fell drunkenly asleep in it, and was moved outside the pub by the others, so that the next morning the good people of Carlow walking past the venue could observe him as he sat there, still semi-comatose in the comfy chair. Indeed, Tony became so attached to the chair, when the place was being sold he asked if he could have it, rather than see it possibly being dumped. He now has it at home, a memento and a trophy of the glory days and glory nights in Scraggs. But even though he got it upholstered, it never feels quite as comfy as it used to.

Morning would come and they would wander off for breakfast to Sally's restaurant, a full Irish after the night's debauchery. Other times on the way home they might pick up a freshly baked loaf of bread from Crotty's bakery, then perhaps an *Irish Independent* from a bundle outside the newsagent's.

Collectively they were given a name by a local 'character', who called them simply 'The Scraggs Bollixes'. It struck such a note of truth with them, they had T-shirts printed bearing the legend, 'Scraggs Bollix On Tour'. They wore these on what became known as their 'away trips', to Duncannon, to Fethard, maybe to Waterford. And then the famous occasion when they went all the way to Canada, a kind of a grand social outing to the city of Brompton to visit a Carlow man, Jim Kehoe, who had settled there. In all, eight people from the Scraggs community descended on Jim for a memorable away trip.

It wasn't exactly *Brideshead Revisited,* but for Tony O'Reilly and his pals it was a time of freedom and friendship, a time when everything seemed to be a great laugh and nothing much could go wrong that couldn't easily be put right, or just forgotten. If a similar bunch of boys were to come together in Carlow today, they would probably carry on no differently, except perhaps in one respect – in Tony's recollections of this time, there are almost no references to gambling. It was something associated more with older men who watched the horse-racing on a Saturday, with the annual nonsense of the Grand National, or with the occasional big football match, maybe the All-Ireland final. Even the money that they used to win or lose in the games of cards in Scraggs seemed like a harmless bit of sport with no darker meaning, certainly with none of the slightly troubling connotations of the man in his early twenties in 2017, sitting at the bar of his local pub, drinking and betting on his smartphone.

In 1993 and 1994 there was no such thing as smartphones. There were the more traditional entertainments of the Republic qualifying for another World Cup, somehow getting the right result against Northern Ireland in the final qualifying match on a horrible, hateful November night in Belfast. And these had been the years, too, in which Ireland couldn't stop winning the Eurovision Song Contest. There was even the odd rumour that the Irish economy might be moving in a better direction after the carnage of the 1980s.

In Carlow, for Tony O'Reilly, everything was fine.

CHAPTER 3

In ordinary terms, Tony was getting along nicely, he even had a car on the road, a blue Nissan Micra that he had bought from his older sister, Sandra. He had rededicated himself to the game of football, winning a lot of cups with Stretford United, training during the week and playing matches on Sundays. He was living at home with his parents, well minded. Then in 1997, at the age of twenty-three, he moved with two friends into a house in Carlow town centre, a 'party' house, a madhouse, but probably no madder than any other house in Ireland at that time inhabited by three freedom-loving men in their early twenties. Yes, he was getting along nicely.

And still ... there were moments, usually after a few drinks too many, which seem in retrospect as signs of some immaturity in his nature, maybe a kind of self-destructive streak. While he was never greatly into the drink, there were times when it got the better of him. At one level he found that drinking with others gave him a sense of belonging, yet that need to belong also suggested an insecurity in him. Of course, that would not have been untypical of any young Irish person given to the odd bout of carousing – and yet Tony would come to be seen as most untypical, so there is always the temptation to look for clues in what may have seemed at the time like harmless indulgence.

He recalls one escapade, a trip to the Heysel Stadium in Brussels in late 1997 for the second leg of the World Cup play-off between the Republic of Ireland and Belgium, the first leg having finished 1–1, the away goal for Belgium meaning that a draw was not a good result for Ireland. He had just returned from the outing to Canada, and was sitting at the counter of the front bar in Scraggs with a few hundred pounds of the holiday money still in his pocket. When a few of the regulars suggested that he might want to go with them to Belgium for the match (leaving more or less straightaway), the fact that he had the few quid on him and the fact that he was up for any devilment anyway led him to say yes.

The only slightly unusual aspect of this particular skite was that the four men he was joining were older than him. In the course of the journey there and back, as with any group of Irish fans at the time, there was much drinking. Indeed, it was a matter of great pride among the Irish that they could drink and still behave themselves. But because these men were essentially better at drinking than Tony, more experienced, he found it hard to stay with the pace. It was as if he felt the need to prove himself, even if it was only on the level of his tolerance for alcohol.

So it was a joyous couple of days, most of the time, with this undercurrent of self-reproach on the part of the boy because he couldn't quite cut it with the men. Or at least that's how he saw it. They were men, and he wasn't quite one of them.

In a café in Brussels, where the locals were not accustomed to such scenes, he remembers the Irish drinking like lords to the extent that the staff just weren't able for it. In the stadium he felt something else, a sadness to be in the Heysel where, as a Liverpool fan watching it on television, he had seen the disaster at the 1985 European Cup final in which thirty-nine people had died.

These memories affected him more than the game itself, which finished 2–1 for Belgium, with Luc Nilis scoring the winner after Luís Oliveira had scored for Belgium and Ray

Houghton had equalised. The defeat was not unexpected, and the members of the delegation from Carlow were still in raucous mood, with one of them becoming embroiled in a dispute with a mounted policeman – all of this taking place as they realised that they would need a taxi because they had missed the bus to the airport.

Somehow, chaotically, the taxi got them to the plane on time, though by this stage Tony realised he had run out of money. Today he will suggest that these wild scenes in which he is constantly trying to keep up with the older men, the 'real' men, may be another indicator of this need in him for affirmation. And he will also recall in mordant tones that vision of himself sitting in that taxi with no money in his pocket, seeing it as a clear example of this other weakness of his, for living beyond his means.

At this time he was also struggling to balance his work life with the serious demands of his football team, a situation that led to a meeting with the manager of Scraggs to try to reach a compromise. Tony suggested that if he took Sundays off, to enable him to play with Streford United, he could do a double shift on Thursdays. This was not acceptable, however, and something else would have to be worked out. On the way out of that meeting, as he walked through the front bar, he had one of those 'chance encounters' that usually happen only in soap operas – the sort of incident that seems trivial at the time, but turns out to have enormous consequences further down the line.

One of the men with whom he had gone to Brussels was a regular for lunch in the front bar of Scraggs. He also happened to be employed in Carlow post office. On this day, as Tony emerged from his inconclusive meeting with his manager, the post office worker was having lunch at the bar. Given the conversation he had just had about his work arrangements,

Tony mentioned to him that if anything came up in the post office, he'd be interested.

A few weeks later, something came up.

It was interesting too that it came up in a way that was strikingly similar to what had happened when the job in Scraggs had come up. Two employees in the Carlow post office had left. A pattern was forming whereby whatever needed to happen to get him successfully to the next phase of his life would duly happen, without him doing very much to cause it.

So, in February 1998 he became a part-time postman. The hours were 7.30 a.m. to 1.30 p.m., five days a week. The contract was a short-term one, lasting seven months, but there was a chance he'd be kept on after that. There was also a chance that he wouldn't.

He knew, though, that if everything went right for him, he had prospects here of a solid job, a career. Having turned down the sugar factory almost on a whim, he felt doubly grateful that this opportunity had fallen to him. On the Sunday before he started, he sprained his ankle playing for Streford United, an injury that would keep anyone from cycling around the town delivering the mail, but one that he was prepared to endure in the circumstances. Instead of calling in sick, he strapped up the injured ankle tightly and put on a pair of Doc Martens in the hope that they would provide whatever support was needed to get him through his round. If all failed, his father was on hand to drive him around the town with the post, door to door, just to get it done.

He got through it somehow, that day, and the next, and pretty soon he was not just healed he was flying fit, due to a combination of the football and the cycling and the fact that he had also given up cigarettes. On many days he was able to finish before the allotted hours were up, because that was the deal – when you were finished with the delivery, the job was done. So he could go home to watch a video, maybe to help his mother, Colette, around the house or to drive her wherever she needed to go. He was giving up rent money at home every week, too. He was in tremendous shape in many ways.

He was still doing Mondays and Tuesdays in Scraggs, after delivering the post – effectively he had moved from a permanent position at Scraggs to this part-time arrangement. Friends told him he was mad to give up a full-time job just for the half-chance that something more permanent might come from the post office. Indeed, there were no guarantees of any kind that he'd be kept on for a single day more than the seven months stipulated in his contract. He decided to take that chance, decided it was worth the gamble. And he was right.

CHAPTER 4

A few months into his time as a part-time postman, Tony, along with a colleague, was called in to the office of the manager and asked if he was interested in 'working on the counters'. In the bureaucratic language of An Post, his grade would still be that of a temporary postman, 'acting up' to a clerical grade. Fortunately, he was suited to such a role. It sounded just right for him given his experience working in Scraggs, managing tills and stocks and dealing with customers.

It seemed that the gods were arranging things in a benign and orderly fashion. He had known there was a chance for such promotion, but now the opportunity had arrived. And if it worked out for him on the counters, not only was it less physically demanding than cycling around Carlow every day, there was the prospect of a permanent position and more money.

And so, as a 'temporary postman acting up', he went for a few weeks' training in Portlaoise, learning about the daily workings of a post office, about counter balances and investment services, saving certificates and stock balances, customer service skills, stamps and postal orders, Western Union money transfers, and cash management in general. He also learned about Riposte, the An Post computer system.

At the end of the course there was an interview conducted by two senior managers, in a formal atmosphere, to get a sense of what sort of person was being taken on by the organisation.

They wanted to see if they had missed anything about the candidate during the training that might lead to problems further up the road. Though it was conducted in a serious way, in suits and ties, Tony recalls that there was a feeling that you had already got the job, that only some major meltdown could stop you at this stage. But there was also a written exam at the end of it all, just to be sure.

This was the part of the procedure in which Tony would remove any doubts about his suitability, allowing him, as it did, to demonstrate his extraordinary skill at writing down whatever was in his head for page after pristine page, with none of the usual blemishes that afflict the vast majority of us – the false starts, the misspellings, the lines crossed out or the words inserted where they should have been in the first place.

When it comes to the written word, Tony's work is always immaculately presented. In more recent times he has been keeping a journal, and it is striking how perfectly put together his thoughts are on the page. It is handwritten, but there are no words crossed out, virtually no mistakes of any kind, it is a perfectly 'clean' document. Yet it has also been written quite quickly, so the neatness and clarity have not been achieved by taking undue care with every detail, or by rewriting after a more messy first draft. It displays a highly developed sense of order that is almost disturbing, as if he is subconsciously keeping a lid on the wilder elements within him, known or unknown. Tony describes it as part of his 'OCD tendencies', but it is very impressive.

While he had had a few strokes of luck in getting to this stage, when the interviewers saw how meticulous he was in these matters, it must have been clear that they too were in luck here. That here was an outstanding candidate.

In order to get some practical experience, Tony went back to Carlow post office for a week, to sit behind the counter observing how it was done, moving from theory into solid practice. Cash management was a big part of it – counting it, making sure you didn't have too much in case of robberies, keeping enough working stock and time-locking the rest. Though as it happened, the Carlow branch was close to the Garda station, and in Tony's time there it was never burgled.

Tony started as the most junior of everyone in Carlow, but that was soon to change for the better. Around 2000, two years after he started with the company, An Post went through a large-scale restructuring and new vacancies opened up, with new working conditions and working hours. He was told that a position was coming up in Dublin, that the process would involve going to work for a period in Dublin and then putting in a request to be transferred back, but that he would then return as a 'duty holder', in other words full-time and pensionable.

He applied and was interviewed again, this time at Fenian Street in the centre of Dublin. He drove up in the Micra, with Niall Byrne along for company. When they reached the vicinity of what should be Fenian Street, they realised they didn't really know how to get there. They were running out of time, and they were lost. As they found themselves going the wrong way down a one-way street, Tony felt that his big day was turning into something out of *Mr. Bean*.

Late for the interview, panicking, Tony jumped out of the car, searching for his destination, leaving Niall, who had only just started learning to drive, to park the car. It was a very hot day, so by the time he found the place he was not just late he was out of breath and sweating, to such an extent that he was told to go downstairs and settle down for a while before the interview.

But this too turned out to have a fortunate aspect, because to some extent it took the tension out of the interview.

Thinking he had screwed it up already, his expectations were lower, so he could respond more naturally. He got the job.

The gods, it seemed, were on his side, even when it looked like they were against him. Even his bad breaks were turning out good.

Now he was driving up and down every day between Carlow and the post office in Tallaght, and he was still working Sunday nights as a DJ in Scraggs, getting about €60 and free drink for the night. For a man in his mid-twenties, this was an excellent state of affairs. The Cure, New Order, Blondie, Pearl Jam, Aztec Camera's 'Somewhere In My Heart', these were the sounds he played, maybe even singing along with them over the mic, while some of the clientele pressed him to play inferior records – a curious reverse of the usual state of affairs whereby the DJ is playing rubbish and the punters want something better. Afterwards he would stay on with the staff, as he had always done, maybe having a crack at the karaoke, which would sometimes leave him struggling to get to work in Dublin on the Monday morning.

Indeed, at one point he was given a verbal warning about this pattern which had developed, whereby he would be absent from work on some Monday mornings and the odd Friday. His fatigue was not always down to carousing in Scraggs. There was a high sick-note rate in general in the Tallaght branch, located at The Square shopping centre. It was known as the office that nobody wanted, because it was one of the busiest in the country. But then that was part of the reason why the vacancy had come up in the first place, so on the whole he had got the better part of that deal too.

But those groggy Monday mornings led to his file being marked with the ominous initials PDP – Possible Drink Problem. He was taken aside and informed of this in a gentle sort of a way by his superior, who rightly felt that this possible problem would not be hard to fix.

This setback was soon put behind him and he continued to move upwards. The restructuring of An Post led to new pay grades being established and new positions being filled around the country. Many in the Carlow branch either got new jobs or took redundancy. At the end of this shakeout, somehow, Tony arrived back down to Carlow to take up a counter position, senior to a lot of people in the office. It wasn't long before he was being interviewed for the position of Acting Branch Manager.

It had eventually come down to a contest between him and one other colleague, and during the interview process it was Tony who moved ahead.

Less than three years from the day that he had started in this branch of An Post as a part-time postman, Tony O'Reilly was now running the establishment. It might be tempting to blame fate for how everything had fallen into place for him, but then, he was highly intelligent, he was very good at the job, and from his years in the pub trade he was good with people too.

Years later, in a court of law, he would be called 'the golden child' because of the speed of his progress up the ranks while he was still in his late twenties and for how everything had worked out so well in his career, which he was enjoying without the slightest inkling of what madness awaited him.

CHAPTER 5

In 2001, Acting Branch Manager Tony O'Reilly was on good money, permanent and pensionable, and still working in his most permanent post of all, in Scraggs. He had no outlays. As a single man living with friends in a rented house in Cathedral Close in the middle of Carlow, he had acquired no mortgages or insurances or any of the other eternal burdens of middle-class existence. He was still able to buy another car from his sister Sandra and give money into the family home.

He was almost bored by the ease of it all. There was the 'Monday night club', which was essentially a drinking session with his friends, and which didn't rule out some socialising on the Tuesday night either. There was the football team. There was work. There was Scraggs. He would sometimes have a bet, say a fiver accumulator on the Saturday football, or €1 on the results of ten games – the classic 'fun bets' as the industry likes to call them. And a few of them clicked, though it was never anything of any consequence. He was still a stranger to the addictive side of it.

The compulsions he had at this time, such as they were, involved spending on CDs, on stereos, on sound equipment, on DVDs, boxsets, a huge television, another computer and clothes. Tony would never be a saver of money.

But his solid sources of income meant it was easy to get any loans he needed. And with his trips to the bookies involving little more than a quick visit to fill in a docket and then straight out the door, his football bets were not a problem in any sense. But he could feel that starting to change.

In the post office in Carlow there was what could be described as a culture of betting. Colleagues would be getting tips for horses, there would be someone who knew someone who heard something about this stable that was coming into form or whatever, all that intrigue of the racing game in which Tony had not been interested, but in which he was starting to get interested, and very interested.

He had always gone downtown for lunch every day, but now he was starting to go from the restaurant to the betting office, and for longer than the two minutes that he used to spend there. He was becoming fascinated by the lingo of the racing punters, listening to them rationalising the results – 'he was pulling the neck off him' … 'he was travelling well' … 'he idled a bit in front' – and while he still couldn't see himself as one of those hardened punters, and certainly not as someone who would do something as apparently laughable as betting on a greyhound race lasting twenty-nine seconds, day after day he was becoming more intrigued by the dynamic of it.

Mainly he would go to the Paddy Power office, but he was also finding himself in Bruce's, Hackett's and Ladbrokes. Slowly he was forming the view that betting on football might give you ninety minutes of value at least, but there was also something to be said for a horse-race because it was over so quick, and for a dog-race, which was over even quicker.

He laughed at what he calls the 'cartoon racing', the Virtual Racing as the industry calls it, with fake horses running in fake races at fake tracks, the outcome decided by some computer, no actual sport taking place but simply the servicing of the needs of the gambler who just can't stop himself betting on something, anything, at that moment. But soon he wasn't laughing at this either. Like many another man in many another betting office who swore he would never be sucked into such nonsense, he would find his hand going into his pocket and taking out some real money, to bet on these unreal events.

Still, he was mostly betting 'normal' amounts, and having 'normal' levels of enjoyment. As a Liverpool fan he has a particular memory of the 2001 UEFA cup final between Liverpool and Alavés, when he had €20 at 9/2 on Gary McAllister to score within the ninety minutes. McAllister scored a penalty. Tony and a post office colleague who had also bet on McAllister to score celebrated their own success and that of Liverpool by drinking the winnings for the night. He would have 'friendly' bets with Niall Byrne on the outcomes of penalty shoot-outs, bets which he invariably lost.

While the betting was becoming a bigger thing in his life than it had been up to now, in other ways he was becoming more settled.

He had met Fiona in the summer of 2002, when she was a student at Carlow Regional. Perhaps inevitably, it happened at the bar of Scraggs. Tony felt strongly enough about her that he gave up his tickets for U2 at Slane so that they could go on a date – which happened to be in a pub across the road from Scraggs, the Dinn Rí. This in itself suggested a seriousness of intent, a desire to be in a quieter place than Scraggs, with its group dynamic.

It developed quite quickly into a serious relationship. Tony recalls that Fiona was a big fan of Aslan, which allowed him to display the extent of his influence by arranging for her to meet the band after they played in Scraggs – a move that was tantamount to a formal and public commitment.

As Tony remembers it, his life was starting to become very settled, very quickly. Niall looks back at that time and marvels at the speed with which Tony changed from being this free-roaming member of the Scraggs 'family', who regularly crashed in his house, into someone contemplating major grown-up issues, such as buying his own house and all that goes into it.

After college Fiona got a job in the offices of a department store in Dublin, which meant that Tony travelled up to the city a couple of times a week, with Fiona down in Carlow at the weekends. He started doing a diploma in Front Line Management at Carlow Regional, a two-year course that would put him in the best possible position if a better job opportunity came up in An Post. Having gone so far in the job, he was still thinking that he could do better.

There were fewer nights with the lads now, less of the all-night carousing in Scraggs. He and Fiona were saving for a house in Sandhills, just a mile from the centre of Carlow, a semi-detached, regular-looking house in which so many irregular transactions would take place. The deal to buy the house went through from start to finish in about a fortnight. Tony moved into it first, living there on his own for a few weeks, doing the garden, sowing grass, putting up sheds, buying furniture. Again, it had been easy enough for him to get a mortgage, with his permanent and pensionable job. Fiona had also received a redundancy payment, which helped towards the down-payment.

In January 2004, they managed to get away to Barcelona for a long weekend to get engaged. He recalls that they went to Camp Nou to see a Barcelona team that featured one Patrick Kluivert, scorer of the first goal that had given him that first winner in 1998. But in Barcelona six years later, even though Kluivert scored on this night too, Tony was getting no flashbacks, no euphoric recall.

Like much that had happened in his twenties, Tony's relationship with Fiona and the life they were starting to build had gone according to what seemed like a pre-ordained plan. It had run smoothly from the start. He had been introduced to her parents quite early and had got on well with them, especially her father, with whom he could talk about horse-racing. He became friendly too with Fiona's brother, Jack, who in 2003 had bought Tony O'Reilly a present that must have seemed utterly innocuous at the time, a perfectly fine present for a man who enjoyed his sport and liked the occasional bet – a €50 voucher for Paddy Power online.

Though he was spending more time at the bookies, too much time perhaps, Tony had never had an online betting account and had only a vague awareness of the concept. But in order to activate the voucher, he would have to go online to register with Paddy Power using his credit card. He was able to do this because he had acquired a Dell PC, along with all the other excellent equipment he had bought, much of which he was still paying for, but he could afford that arrangement.

On 22 February 2003, Tony O'Reilly of 10, Sandhills, Carlow, Co. Carlow, set up an account with Paddy Power using his driving licence as ID and choosing the username Tony 10.

It was a lucky number for him, 10, a significant number in various ways. It was the number on the shirt he wore when playing for Stretford United, it was the title of Pearl Jam's first album, and he had even favoured the house in Sandhills because it was number 10.

The setting up of the online account did not change him into a high roller, it didn't have a sudden and massive impact on his life. He was focused on his career, on Fiona, on their new life together, so he continued to bet in a recreational way – just to have an interest.

A year later, in the summer of 2004, he had what he

considered at the time to be his first serious bet online. He had received some reliable information that Rafael Benitez was about to be made the next manager of Liverpool. The 'Next Manager' markets are generally regarded as a place to which only fools would venture, but in this case the information was so solid that it made the odds of Evens seem highly attractive.

Tony put €100 on it, at Evens, on Betfair. Benítez indeed became the manager of Liverpool. It was a particularly sweet winner because Tony had agonised so much over it, not just because it was a strange market for him but because of the size of the stake.

In 2004 he was betting €100 and thinking it was huge money.

PART 2

CHAPTER 6

On the day that he opened his online account with Paddy Power in February 2003, Tony O'Reilly had a bet of 1 euro. By the day that his account was closed, in June 2011, he had staked ten million, four hundred and ninety thousand, four hundred and sixty euro, and sixty-six cents.

That's just under €10.5 million, in the account of one man, using one website.

That number is there, on the first page of a document that was eventually released by the Paddy Power corporation, listing a full account of every bet placed by Tony 10, under the heading 'Total Staked'.

€10490460.66

There is no comma after the 10, so you might at first glance think that it is a million and something, not ten million and something. Indeed, without the comma it has the vague look of a bank account number, or something technical like an IP address, related to a computer not a person. It might as well have been, given that a stake of 1 euro could ultimately lead to a combined stake of more than ten million euro.

And that was just the number for the Sportsbook, which was where Tony 10 mainly lived, racking up a total of 6,272 bets along the way. There is also a Games and Casino total of €70178, a Wagerworks Casino total of €270434.9, and a Live Casino number of €5455. There's a figure of €1208 for 'Lotteries'.

Altogether it is north of €300,000, but really this seems like an afterthought next to the main event, which was usually happening with the horse-racing or the football or the tennis, or whatever happened to be on in the world of sports betting at any given moment in the life of Tony 10 in the years between 2003 and 2011.

But there is another number, just under the 'Total Staked' of €10413619.66, that is equally mesmerising. That number is €9013035.03 under 'Total Winnings'.

That would be the nine million, thirteen thousand and thirty-five euro and three cents won by Tony 10, and that is an awful lot of winning. Though eventually it must be acknowledged that it leaves an overall loss of €1400584.63, or one million, four hundred thousand, five hundred and eighty-four euro and sixty-three cents. And that is an awful lot of losing.

When you hear a spokesperson from one of the betting corporations talking on the radio, you will sometimes hear the line that their ideal client is one who stakes €100 and who wins back €90, leaving a nice margin of €10 for the bookie and a bit of fun for the punter and no harm done.

In the case of Tony O'Reilly, the ratio was working out roughly in this way, except you'd need to multiply it by about 10,000 to get near the truth.

The full betting history of this man, who worked in the post office and who had no other legitimate source of income in all this time, amounts to 660 pages, a bit like one of those Tribunal reports that are read by about four people, but which tell us of terrible things if only we had the heart to read them. So it is with this document, which, when opened at random near the end, at page 595, records a €20,000 accumulator on five tennis matches featuring players known only to aficionados. And that €20,000 accumulator is just one of numerous bets on that day, with stakes such as €17,000, €25,000, €30,000.

That is indeed awe-inspiring when you view this page on its own, but if you have read through the previous 594 pages, by the time you reach this one you have become so accustomed to these astronomical numbers, you no longer see them as real. Instead, you tend to see them as just numbers, somehow unrelated to the human being who is generating them, and how he might have done that, and his state of mind at the time.

He didn't start out like that, though, and he certainly didn't intend to end up like that. That's clear on the opening day of this astonishing journey, where that bet of 1 euro is listed. It is not the only bet on that day, but it stands there as if it's seeking your attention, so ridiculously small it seems as surreal, in its own way, as a €20,000 accumulator on five bad tennis matches.

You couldn't make it up – that a man would start at a euro and build to ten million, but it is there: one euro, on page one.

Tony had gone through his €50 Paddy Power gift voucher in a couple of losing football bets on Southampton and Barcelona. Then he made a deposit of €10, the first online bet he would make using his own money. And perhaps it was a sign of some subconscious foreboding on his part, but he broke this €10 into four separate bets of €1, €2, €2 and €5, on Michael Owen to score for Liverpool. As if he still wasn't sure how the online system worked, or didn't trust it.

He lost that one, and a week later he made a deposit of €40, which he also lost in bets on horses, followed by deposits of €20 and €15 and another €20, until finally he got a winner when Henrik Larsson scored for Celtic, resulting in the first withdrawal to his credit card of €55.

This is all recorded on the first page of this enormous document, but it must be noted that the betting takes place over a period of two months, that the biggest single bet is €40 and that many of them are less than a tenner, and therefore there is nothing to be concerned about here. Certainly, Tony was not in any way concerned – rather than getting gung-ho after his first win, when he withdrew the €55 he had won, he replaced it with a deposit of just €15.

At this stage it looks no more than a recreation, hardly even an enthusiasm, with very little traffic on the site for the rest of that year. It even includes the odd 'novelty' bet, which is the mark of the unserious punter – though it must be said that the €10 he had on Miss Ireland Rosanna Davison to win the Miss World beauty pageant in December 2003 returned a triumphant €60.

A small flag might be raised by the fact that he made a deposit at around noon on Christmas Day 2003, but Tony is a football man and there's a lot of football on at this time of year, and it was only €20, a tenner on two accumulators. These are the sort of numbers we are looking at, very little above two figures, not much to suggest that here was a man chasing the buzz he had got a few years back with his first big win. It speaks more of a man involved at a modest level with that daily gambling culture he had found among his work colleagues.

Tony himself remembers it like this, as no more remarkable than the punting of any man or woman with an easily affordable betting habit. Indeed, two years after he had opened the online account he was still capable of having a bet of €3 on a horse. And on the rare occasion when he might stray into three figures – like when he got that information about Rafa Benítez becoming manager of Liverpool – it would not involve much more than €100 and it was clearly a response to some such tip that was going round, because it wouldn't be repeated for a while.

He was having some nice winners, too. One of those rare three-figure bets was put on a horse called *Fire Dragon*, which returned €600. A bet of €50 on José-Antonio Reyes to score returned €350 and a €10 treble on the horses returned €220. Most of these winnings were withdrawn quickly and replaced by a much smaller deposit.

He didn't feel that he was in any sort of trouble, other than the regular existential troubles of boredom that tend to arrive when a person's life becomes more settled. Yet he had worked so hard for this too, to achieve such stability, and he was still ambitious enough to be doing that college course in Front Line Management.

There is, perhaps, the odd indication that this might be turning into something more than a harmless bit of sport. Towards the end of March 2005, in a space of just over two hours one afternoon, there are sixteen transactions involving deposits, withdrawals and bets on horses – most of them no more than a fiver or tenner, but still a significant amount of activity, a lot of boredom there to be killed.

On 6 May there are twenty-one transactions, starting with a deposit of €20 at three minutes to eight in the morning, and ending with a glorious withdrawal of €600 on the last race of the evening when *Byron Bay* returns €720 for a stake of €60.

The following day is busy too, and again there is an outstanding winner: a bet of €100 on *Tiber Tiger* returning €700, and resulting in a withdrawal of €650. No sign, then, that Tony 10 is leaving any largish amount in his online account. He is resisting that temptation, taking away his winnings and starting again with a deposit that is usually €50.

On the evening of 8 May, sitting with his sister Sandra in the front bar of Scraggs, he watches Ronaldinho scoring first for Barcelona, which gives Tony 10 another cracking result: a return of €800 for a stake of €100, and a withdrawal of €700.

Something else is happening now, though, some new energy is entering the game, because on 9 May there is a deposit of €200, the biggest yet, all of which is placed on a horse called *Just A Try*, for which he had a tip from someone in the post office. *Just A Try* wins, with a return of €1,500. None of it is withdrawn.

◆ ◆ ◆

To this day, Tony still can't point to anything that was going on in his life at this time, any friction with friends or colleagues or with Fiona, anything at all of a negative nature that was causing him to change his behaviour, to shut himself off, to get a little bit deeper into the gambling. Indeed, it was mostly a positive thing that was drawing him in just a bit further, the pleasure of winning. It was just the gambling itself, creating its own energy, its own momentum. These withdrawals of very decent amounts, such as €650 or €700, were telling him that not only was he in no danger here, he might even have found a viable alternative source of income, or at least a way of paying off his credit card.

It was the gambling itself that was making it happen.

When you read through this document, trying to fathom the magnitude of it, the picture it is building of a man slowly and terribly going down, there are many points at which you want to press the proverbial pause button, to call a halt to it right now, to re-imagine this story if the betting had stopped at a certain point, and the first such point is 9 May 2005.

Despite the victories – indeed because of them – you wish that this month of May in general had not happened for Tony O'Reilly, you want to edit it out of his life somehow, to start again and to send him abroad for a few weeks or something that might shift him in a different direction.

But it is there, it is done, and it cannot be undone.

That €1,500 he had in his account after *Just A Try* obliged is the first substantial amount that stays in his account. There is no withdrawal, not even of a few hundred, and it all goes down the following day in quite large bets – one of €300 – on various horses. All of them lose. By teatime he has nothing in his account. He makes a fresh deposit of €100.

And yet this month is not about losing, it is mainly about winning.

The numbers are starting to rise, but apparently in a good way. On 14 May at 2.22 p.m. there's a bet of €250 on a horse called *Far Pavilions*, which returns €1,374. Ten minutes later there's a bet of €1,000 on *Rakti*, which returns €2,662.

That's a bet of €1,000, a grand. The man who once thought it appropriate to wager €1 is now betting a grand on a horse.

As Tony remembers it, he was in a pub at the time, near Citywest, with a friend of his, a man who loved the horses. Fiona and the man's partner had gone into Dublin, so the two men settled into an afternoon in the pub, betting on the racing at Newbury. In that atmosphere of happy indulgence, with a decent balance in his account, it seemed to make sense to Tony 10 to have his first four-figure bet online, on the temperamental but high-class six-year-old *Rakti* in the Lockinge Stakes.

Rakti led the race for most of the way and went clear to win by five lengths, providing his supporters at the bar in Citywest with just about the perfect betting experience. At the end of that afternoon Tony 10's account has €3,600 in total. As if to demonstrate that he was still in control of this thing, he withdraws €2,000.

The following day there is another excellent winner when Julio Baptista scores for Real Madrid. Tony withdraws €1,950. He is a man in charge of his own destiny. The numbers are rising for Tony 10, but mainly to his benefit. It is going well, and it is about to get even better.

CHAPTER 7

One of the tabloid newspapers used to do a feature on Monday mornings listing the various sports results from over the weekend and revealing how fantastically rich a punter would now be if he or she had put all these results into an accumulator. The key to it was the fact that none of these results was greatly unexpected or freakish in any way. Indeed, they all seemed perfectly obvious now that it was Monday morning and you'd somehow 'lost' this great investment that you hadn't had the courage, or even just the basic common sense, to make.

Looking back, it so often seems obvious. Just as it did to Tony O'Reilly in the days after he won almost €5,000 with a €50 double on CSKA Moscow to win the UEFA Cup and Bobby Zamora to score first for West Ham in the second leg of the 'play-off' semi-final against Ipswich Town.

This was the one.

This was the bet, on the evening of 18 May 2005, which brought him all the way back to that feeling of absolute euphoria he had experienced when Patrick Kluivert had scored the first goal and Holland had beat Argentina 2–1.

This was the one that changed everything. He is quite clear about this. He did not get such a feeling even when he'd had a grand on *Rakti* and it won in a canter. No, it was the double on Zamora and CSKA Moscow that sent him into the next dimension.

He had arrived home from work to the house he shared with Fiona in Sandhills with the intention of looking at the second half of the UEFA Cup final between Sporting Lisbon and CSKA Moscow, perhaps switching from time to time to the second leg of that play-off semi-final between Ipswich Town and West Ham, which was tied at 2–2 after the first leg. He'd had a few losses on various horses that day. Starting in the late afternoon, in just over an hour he had dropped a total of €450. Still, he had no major intentions of getting it all back on the football – though he had seen CSKA Moscow in previous rounds of the competition and been most impressed by them. The matches had started by the time he got home. He went straight into the shower, still intending to just watch the second half.

He came down from the shower and was still drying himself as he checked out the Paddy Power site on his laptop. He was surprised to find that Sporting Lisbon were leading 1–0, but then, unusually, the final was being played on their home ground, the Estádio José Alvalade. He still fancied CSKA Moscow because, despite the strangely poor record of Russian teams in general in European competitions, this CSKA side had some high-class players in Carvalho, Zhirkov and Olić. And they had got to this final in some style, with their striker, Vágner Love, in particular having a terrific season.

A goal down at half-time, they were now 10/1 to win the game. Tony felt that looked like good value. His attention then shifted to the odds of 8/1 being offered 'in-running' on Bobby Zamora to score the first goal against Ipswich, in a game that was scoreless at half-time, still 2–2 on aggregate. Being a striker himself, Tony liked the look of that too. He sensed that Zamora was in form. And while the bet demanded not only that Zamora would score but that he would score the first goal, the striker in form will tend to get the goal that is most needed, will be able to cope with that pressure.

It also came to Tony's attention that a free bet had dropped into his account, one of those odd little gifts that the betting corporations bestow from time to time, to show their appreciation. All in all, the gods seemed to be ordaining it.

After losing that €450 so quickly in the afternoon he might have felt reluctant to start betting again when he got home, if it hadn't been for that free bet arriving, giving him the sense that he had ammunition in reserve. At 8.21 p.m. he made a deposit of €50, and at 8.22 p.m. he went for the double of CSKA Moscow to win the game and Bobby Zamora to score the first goal. The combined odds on both of these things happening within the next forty-five minutes was not far off 100/1. And still it seemed to make sense.

Just after half-time in the Estádio José Alvalade, there is a moment in the game that should have brought the bet down, swiftly and decisively, reducing all of Tony's fine calculations to nothing, mocking them. Sporting Lisbon are still dominating, a ball flies past Akinfeev, the Moscow keeper, yet somehow it rebounds back to him off a Sporting player. It's a ridiculous escape for the Russians, and of course for Tony O'Reilly, who also has to endure the sight of a free-kick from Rochemback for Lisbon hitting the bar. Then, as if sensing that this is their destiny, CSKA proceed to hit the Portuguese with what one report described as 'an almighty sucker punch'. It is a header from the defender Berezutski from a free-kick on the right delivered precisely by Daniel Carvalho.

It's 1–1, just ten minutes into the second half, and CSKA are hitting their stride, as Tony rightly felt they would. And so are West Ham, and in particular one Bobby Zamora.

Five minutes after the CSKA equaliser, Tony is checking out the play-offs action. Marlon Harewood goes on a powerful run down the right and squares the ball past the Ipswich keeper for Zamora to put it into the empty net from six yards.

The first part of the double is up. Zamora will score again in the game and West Ham will win 4–2 on aggregate, but none of that matters now to Tony. When Zamora got that crucial first goal, he had done his job for the night.

There is now €50 at 8/1 going on CSKA Moscow at 10/1. To be precise, there's a stake of €450 to be possibly multiplied by ten, which would yield an overall return of €4,950.

CSKA are flying. A few minutes later they are on the break after a Sporting attack, and Carvalho again slips a perfect pass to Zhirkov, who puts it under the body of the keeper, Ricardo. It is 2–1 to CSKA. If the game stops now, there's nearly five grand waiting for Tony O'Reilly, but the game will go on for another thirty minutes or so, with Sporting now starting to get desperate, seeing it slipping away from them when it was all looking so fine.

For Tony, the sooner it can slip away from them, the better. And not only does that happen, he has to wait just another ten minutes for CSKA to score a third, the killer goal coming from Vágner Love, after it was laid on for him again by the man of the match, Carvalho.

The glorious vision for Sporting, of winning their first European trophy on their own ground, evaporates. But in this world in which so many things are so madly interconnected, their failure has not only given the Russians an equally rare moment of ultimate European victory, it has made a profound difference to the life of a man sitting in a house in Carlow, in Ireland.

Tony O'Reilly is going to collect almost €5,000 for an investment of €50, a victory based not on some freak of nature but on his own judgement, his shrewd assessment of the games and of the odds. And though about a hundred other things still had to go right for him after he made that call, and all these things were entirely beyond his control, it still feels as if he made his own luck here. It feels like he has become good enough at this thing to weigh up the evening's football and to make the right calls and to find himself, less than an hour later, with a profit of about five grand. No, this hadn't been wild guesswork on his part, it had been highly educated guesswork, giving him the deep feeling of satisfaction of a man who has won big, not just because he is lucky, like some Lotto winner, but because he is smart too.

He is utterly elated, more so than when he had the much larger bet on *Rakti*. There was something about the way the pieces all fell in his favour in the second half of both matches that had an almost mystical dimension, as if the pieces of his meticulous personality had also come together at last, and he had finally found the thing that he was really good at, finally found himself.

◆ ◆ ◆

The following morning at 7.52 a.m. he withdraws €2,000 of the €4,950 from his account.

That afternoon he starts again, with a bet of €50 on a horse called *Mullaad* that returns €350, then another €50 on *Princess Kiotto*, which also obliges, returning €217. Over the next three days he makes three separate withdrawals of €1,000.

It seems that he can't stop winning.

CHAPTER 8

While 2005 is going well in terms of bets rolling in his favour, winning the big double has not made Tony rich. Indeed, overall he is struggling with his finances, requiring the occasional loan from the credit union or Bank of Ireland to keep the gambling going along with everything else. He and Fiona have a mortgage on the house at Sandhills, and though she is still working their two incomes are hardly enough to cover all the costs of moving into the new place – along with the quiet drain through which money is starting to move from Tony's side to the website of Paddy Power.

These loans would only have been a grand, or maybe two grand, but even in this more modest phase of gambling, Tony has managed to max out a credit card with a limit of €5,000. And while such loans would not have been at all unusual at a time in Ireland when the banks were virtually pleading with all-comers to borrow as much as they liked, with this need to keep topping up, Tony can feel the pressure starting to build.

There is another pressure, which he hardly even noticed at the time – the fact that he needs to keep all of this to himself. All the betting, all the winning and the losing, and the borrowing, are taking place in this sealed world occupied only by him – unless you count the corporate entity that is Paddy Power. Tony insists that even those closest to him, including Fiona, who would have been most aware of his daily comings and goings, had not the slightest idea of the obsession that

was starting to grow in him. Anyone with experience in this
area would believe him on this, and believe her too, because
that is how it works – there is this astonishing silence that the
gambler is able to maintain in order to keep it all going, to
stay in the game, somehow.

He is getting clever about it, too, knowing that he can't
simply deny that he is spending quite a lot of time engaged
in sports betting on some level. Certainly, a lot of it can
be explained by his obvious love of sport in general and
football in particular, but he is careful also to admit to
some extravagance on the punting side, to make it all seem
credible. So when he wins that five grand on Zamora and
CSKA Moscow, he tells Fiona he has won about €800, which
by an excellent coincidence is roughly what she needs to
complete some dental work she has been undergoing. It helps
to create an impression that this gambling thing could yield
the occasional windfall to help the family finances along, and
is otherwise pretty harmless.

Fiona would later have a feeling of embarrassment that is
quite common among those who have lived with a gambler, a
sense of amazement that she never noticed these changes taking
place in Tony, a concern that others might also find it incredible
– 'surely you must have noticed something?' But then, if loved
ones were able to notice such things, and do something about
them, as they can do with alcohol or drugs, gambling would
not be spoken about as the invisible compulsion, and thus the
most intractable one. Indeed, there's a sense in which a wife or
a husband may be too close to see things that others who are
more casually connected may notice, that the gambler is going
to be most guarded at home.

In May 2005, when something changed at a fundamental
level, there is still not a thing that Tony can recall, no rows
he had at home with Fiona or at work, no other troubles,

nothing but the gambling itself that is drawing him into its maw. So in telling his story, the stuff of 'ordinary life' tends to drift into the background, until it is hardly there at all. In truth, another life was starting for Tony 10, and by its nature it could not be shared with anyone.

So he would go to work in the post office in Carlow, and he would come home from work, and the routine never changed. But he was becoming increasingly bored with it, now that he'd finished his management course in the Regional, and now that something else had emerged to consume his energies – even if, unlike the permanent and pensionable job, this latest thing is requiring the occasional trip to the credit union or the bank.

There is that credit card, too, which he is using to deposit funds to his Tony 10 account, and withdraw them, and here too this sudden surge in winnings has not cleared everything. But it has shown him a way to get there, or at least, that is what he feels at the time.

It seems that all gamblers who are becoming addicted are struck by this notion at some stage, this happy vision based on the apparently simple premise that the more money you put on, the more you take out – indeed, could anything be simpler than that? As simple as … if you can win nearly five grand for a stake of €50, maybe you should be staking more than €50. There is absolutely nothing wrong with the logic here, there's no denying that ancient line in the punter's playbook: 'if you don't speculate, you don't accumulate'.

But alas, gambling being what it is, for some maddening reason even the most perfect logic can get all mangled up by the stuff that actually happens on the racetrack or in a game of football.

◆ ◆ ◆

It's there, once again, in the document charting his bets. It's clear now that the numbers are getting bigger. They say it's the hope that kills you, which of course it does. But with gambling it is not just the hope, it is also seeing your hopes realised that kills you. And in the baffling nature of this beast, the most awful moments tend to arrive when Tony wins, and wins big.

For the next month, Tony keeps speculating larger amounts, and accumulating larger amounts. It is the accumulating that makes the heart sink as you read it. Looking at these deposits in which numbers such as €500 are increasingly common, these bets of €400, €500 or €600, the odd €1,000, quite a few of them lose, but then here it comes – a €600 double on the horses returns nearly €4,000. A single bet of €500 on a horse returns €2,750. A by-now relatively modest €100 double returns €1,925.

A lot of bets are going down too, but then Tony is bailed out again by one of these magical winners: a €500 single on a horse called *Balletomaine* that returns €3,750, a grand on *Ginger Spice* that returns €3,250. So in this counter-intuitive way you are thinking: Ah, if only they had all lost … if only these winners hadn't kept supplying the ammunition to keep him going.

It is getting well into July now, and not only is the volume of bets increasing, the balance in his account is starting to look impressive. On 23 July there are twenty-eight transactions, starting at about 1.30 in the afternoon and ending at just before 9.00 in the evening.

He knows he is getting in deeper, and there are moments when the worries start nagging at him. He has a dog called Jack, a creature of many parts, the most obvious of which is cocker spaniel, and while he is walking Jack through the grounds of the Presentation College, Tony is starting to think that maybe he needs to cut down on this, that he's doing fine now, but it could take a few wrong turns too.

He is still flying, though, and the balance in his account is still rising. It is €5,000, then €6,000, then €6,500, then €7,000, and even with some heavy withdrawals it is still heading north, it is €8,500, it is €9,625. Finally, at close of business on 25 July, a bet of €500 on *Dasher Reilly*, ridden by Nina Carberry in a two-mile National Hunt flat race on the first evening of the Galway festival, returns €2,000. All of which leaves Tony 10 with a fine big total of €11,500 in his account.

That evening he is having a pint with Niall Byrne in the snug in the front bar of Scraggs, talking about this good run he's been having lately, without mentioning any specifics. Niall reminds him that he's talking a lot these days about the odds and so forth, tells him he'd need to be careful not to get sucked into the gambling. Tony hears what his friend is saying, and as he sits there in the snug, he thinks that now … now is the time to get out.

Tony is feeling invincible, the endorphins are nearly bursting out of him, but he wants to be smart about this too, he wants to keep his head. He knows that €11,500 would pay off everything he owes – the credit union and bank loans, the credit card. He calculates that not only has he won enough to remove all these pressures, he will still have at least a grand left over for a holiday.

He goes to bed that night convinced that this is the right thing to do, delighted that he has won so much, but knowing that this could easily change. As he drifts off to sleep on the night of 25 July 2005, Tony O'Reilly has the easy mind of a man who has been gambling a lot more than he ever thought he would, but who has found a way out of it – the best way, indeed, with everything back to zero and no harm done, and even a few quid for himself. He figures that he and Fiona might go to Greece, courtesy of Paddy Power.

But he doesn't say anything about this, because he never talks about his gambling, so he keeps that to himself, too, waiting for some opportune time.

That time never comes.

He is forgetting one thing, or at least he is not giving sufficient weight to the fact that the following day the Galway festival is still on, and it will be on for three more days after that.

And that, as it turns out, is most unfortunate.

◆ ◆ ◆

In the post office on the Tuesday morning, the talk is all of Galway, of various tips and hunches and fancies for the evening meeting. It was this betting culture that first drew Tony to the offices of Paddy Power and BoyleSports and Bruce Betting, just to sample the attractions of the daily horse-racing and the dogs and their virtual equivalents. And now that he has gone a lot deeper into it, this office is a difficult place to be for a man who has just resolved to give all that up, and to give it up today.

Maybe not today after all, he thinks. Maybe another day, after Galway.

Anyway, given that he is in a rich vein of form, there seems every chance that he will make more money, that along with the holiday he will be able to buy stuff for the house. He's just making the most of this good run before getting out of it for good.

At lunchtime he uses his phone to place a bet of €500 on *Lasquini Du Moulin*, which is running in the 5.35 p.m. at Galway. The old juices are flowing again. There are two other meetings on that afternoon, at Glorious Goodwood and Beverly, and as if warming up for the evening's hostilities, just after 4.00 p.m. he phones in another €500 on *Iskander*, which is running in the 4.20 p.m. at Beverly, ridden by Nina Carberry. She is the jockey who rode Tony's last winner the previous night at Galway, and she has now travelled over to Beverly for this Dorothy Laird Memorial Ladies Handicap – not a great race, but since Nina is a great jockey, it seems like a reasonable investment on the 2/1 favourite.

She finishes fourth, the €500 goes down, but there is still plenty of 'ammunition' in his account, so he is not greatly concerned. He places a sporting €100 on *My Native Lad* in the 5.00 p.m. race at Galway, the first of the evening. Ridden by Paul Carberry, brother of Nina, it is an 8/1 shot, which is in the lead approaching the last, but which, according to the *At The Races* analyst, was 'soon headed and kept on one-paced'.

Still, Tony has some good information about *Major Title* in the big race of the evening at Galway, so he has €500 on *Major Title* at a price of 9/1. It will turn out that *Major Title* is 'always towards rear, never a factor'.

He gets €500 back when his first bet, on *Lasquini Du Moulin*, is declared void, the horse a non-runner. Then €400 goes on *Eskimo Jack* in the 5.35 p.m., the second favourite at odds of 11/4. *Eskimo Jack* 'disputed lead from three out, headed before last, dropped to third and no impression under pressure from before straight'.

Tony is still in the post office, making the bets and trying to follow the proceedings on his phone. Somewhere in the back of his brain he is hearing the judgement of Ted Walsh, that if you want to go to Galway, 'you should take out a five-pound note and set fire to it, just to see if you can stand the pain'.

But Tony 10 is not that far behind, relatively speaking, and he still sees plenty of opportunities to get it back. He switches to Glorious Goodwood for the 5.45 p.m., and has €500 on *Ridge Boy*, the 13/2 favourite in a very open race. It finishes third, another bet down.

Just after 6.00 p.m. he has €1,000 on *Oodachee* in the 6.10 p.m. at Galway. Ridden by Michael Kinane, it is the 11/4 favourite, so a win here will leave Tony comfortably ahead again. *Oodachee* 'chased leaders, improved into second and ridden approaching straight, soon no impression under pressure, kept on at same pace' and finished fourth.

Tony remembers well how he checked this on his phone just before leaving the office, and how his heart sank. The man who had started the day feeling in control of things, in a position to pay off everything, wondering what he would do with his nice profit, is now no longer in that position. But he feels that he can't stop now. That he is chasing.

To be chasing is a thing that no punter wants. It is this terrible feeling of trying to get back to where you started, yet knowing in the core of your being that you may end up in a worse place than you have ever been.

Tony's got this feeling now, after the blow of *Oodachee* losing him a grand, perhaps the grand he was going to use for that holiday in Greece. He gets home around 7.00 p.m., the Galway races are on television. This is better than trying to keep track of things in the post office. Here, he is in control of his environment. He gets out his laptop, and he places a grand on the 7/2 second favourite in the 7.35 p.m. race, *Mrs. Snaffles*. Again, at these odds a win here and he is free.

The *At The Races* analyst puts it like this: 'led and disputed, ridden to challenge and lead under one furlong out, strongly pressed close home and headed on line'. To put it another way, *Mrs. Snaffles* was beaten by a short head. She was caught on the line by *Chennai*, a 7/1 shot.

A short head – the difference between utter elation for Tony, and savage disappointment.

Still chasing, chasing, chasing, he has €600 on *Gavemers*, who is nowhere. On the last race of the evening he has a grand on *Happy To Chat*, the 11/8 favourite ridden by Pat Shanahan and trained by Dermot Weld, who wins so many races at Galway – but not this one, in which he finishes second.

Tony wasn't going for a big price here, just the sensation of winning again, of getting something back, but it is not to be.

The carnage on the track goes on into the night. Just after 10.00 p.m., Tony moves into the badlands of the American racing, with bets of €200, €500, and two final desperate plays of €1,000 each, all going down. There is perhaps some gallows humour creeping in here, with horses' names such as *Lord of Loot* and *Joke's On Me*.

In the time between the Galway Races and the American action, some small relief comes from an unlikely source, with Tony somehow extracting a profit of roughly €1,500 out of various bets on Liverpool against FC Kaunas in the qualifying round of the Champions League. But on the day on which he was supposed to get out of the betting game, Tony loses €6,500 overall. He withdraws €2,000, as if to hide it from himself, a poignant remnant of the €11,500 he thought he might be withdrawing.

By lunchtime the following day, he has lost another three grand on the horses. By early afternoon he is depositing the €2,000 he withdrew the previous night.

Galway is in its third day, and he is still chasing.

CHAPTER 9

There is a rhythm to it now, almost a routine. On the Sunday after that devastating Galway meeting he has two very good winners. He has €1,500 on *Punctilious* to win at Newbury, which returns €4,000, and he puts a grand on *Balakan* at Cork, also returning €4,000.

The next day, backing horses throughout the afternoon, he loses €6,000.

To tell the story of Tony O'Reilly in cartoon form, you could go for the simplest image of all: a man walking into the sea and continuing to walk despite the fact that the water is rising all the time and he is slowly being consumed by it, yet still he walks, as if unaware of his predicament.

There is almost something methodical about it, a thoroughness about the daily commitment that makes you think of those compulsive tendencies of his in other areas – the need to have all his CDs neatly stacked and in the right order, the desire to have the latest computer or television, or just to buy stuff that he can barely afford, the neatness of the handwriting in his journals. There is an obsessive element in these relatively harmless activities that is now being inflamed by the gambling. Indeed, there is probably no more dangerous place for even the mildly obsessive individual to be than in a gambling environment, with its hyper-addictive energies, the way the players become utterly absorbed in it, the seduction of the tantalisingly possible.

As to where the obsessions or compulsions might be coming from in the first place, in general we are told that they are ways of dealing with some greater anxieties, the nature of which usually emerges only after a long time in therapy or counselling. But in these times in which he is slowly walking into the deepest waters, such things are very far from the mind of Tony O'Reilly.

For now, the only way to gain an understanding of the world, and to feel right about himself, is through gambling. And to keep that going he is increasingly indifferent to the consequences. To keep Tony 10 in business, there is not much left now for Tony O'Reilly, whoever he used to be. From now on, his identity is defined by that username in the top left-hand corner of his Paddy Power account, that is who he is, that is where he lives, that is his name, Tony 10.

The MBNA credit card limit shifts from €5,000 to €10,000. Every couple of months now he is topping up the loans from the credit union or the bank, at a time when, for example, you could make a phone call to Banking365 and have a new loan approved, with the money arriving into your account within a couple of hours.

This thing called ordinary life is still going on for him, or perhaps going on around him, this place in which he is obliged to spend some time before immersing himself again in this other world that has claimed him – and that he must somehow subsidise with his earnings from the post office.

Fiona is usually up first, she has to be gone by 7.30 a.m. to get to work on time. After a shower and a breakfast of tea and toast, Tony 10 cycles to the post office, like any man of relatively modest means who can't quite stretch to a second car, but who is seeing increasingly large sums of money flowing in and out of his betting account.

The cycling might seem like a form of respite from all that, but in truth it is always on his mind. By 8.45 a.m. he is in the post office, getting things ready for the day, which is usually busy in itself, as might be expected in the main post office in a large town, but which is getting more and more demanding for Tony 10 due to this parallel world he inhabits.

Throughout the day he will be using his phone to make bets and to check results. He is starting to buy a lot of scratch cards. There is no smartphone, but he has a Nokia he can use to ring up the bookie with his bets and it just about has the capacity to gain access to the internet, to connect him to the Paddy Power website. He will often go to the toilet to avoid drawing attention to himself when he is engaging in these transactions, and none of his colleagues has any awareness that there is anything in particular going on, that might give them cause for concern.

Yes, there was a gambling culture among them, but Tony 10 is also getting very good at hiding the evidence of his own gambling culture, with his quick mind and his fast-talking manner he is somehow able to control this part of his personality at least. He is a senior figure in the office too, so it is more in the order of things for him to be noting the movements of others.

The 11 a.m. break will often be spent in Hackett's betting office, getting started on the day's punting. At lunchtime he and a colleague might get a sandwich in the Newsworld deli, which they will take to Scraggs to have with a cup of tea. But even here he will have a gambling opportunity of sorts, the tea and sandwiches being a lesser attraction than the *Who Wants To Be A Millionaire?* machine.

Back at the post office counter he is starting to break some of the rules. He is buying scratch cards from his own stock, throwing in a tenner here and there and scratching the cards just to keep his mind busy. He could get sacked for this, but he does it anyway, because of this constant sense of urgency he is feeling, this pathological need that is growing in him.

Distracted though he might be, he is also working hard, keeping it together, dealing with customers, one of whom buys a scratch card off a colleague and wins €20,000 right there at the counter. The best that Tony 10 has managed is a couple of hampers worth about €500, but in this, as in the more sophisticated forms of gambling, it is the process as much as the outcome that is inveigling him in.

His main online account is with Paddy Power, but he is also discovering what he regards as the superior design of the bet365 website. Its soothing colours of black, grey and green seem to appeal to the eye of the gambler in a most seductive way when he is watching an event unfolding, or rather, watching the odds on an event unfolding.

Now he is becoming something of a connoisseur of the way that the betting is 'suspended' on a football match, the moment that the action stops on bet365, the pure adrenaline that runs through him while he is waiting for the next thing to happen, the next goal, or maybe just a near miss that is revealed when the excruciating tension of these moments is finally lifted.

And somehow, while he is spending all this time 'in the zone', he has to keep the people of Carlow supplied with stamps and postal orders, envelopes and savings certificates and dog licences. On his walks with Jack through the grounds of the Presentation College he should be clearing his mind of the multitude of matters that are weighing down on him, but most of the time all he can think about is the day's racing, either glorying in the relief of some victory that has rescued him again, or mourning another appalling defeat.

He and Fiona are planning to get married in May 2007. They have decided to have the wedding in Cyprus, an arrangement that is being paid for in instalments of roughly €600 every few months, with the final bill to be settled in

Cyprus after the event. So this is another payment that he simply must make regardless of any other outgoings on the horses or the football – and anyway, to fail in this might draw unwelcome attention to those outgoings, and to the relative lack of incomings.

There's a particularly narrow escape on the day when they are due to fly to Lanzarote for a holiday. Tony has a tip for a horse called *Run For Paddy* in the Scottish Grand National. It will be a big price, at least 20/1. He does not plan to have a huge amount on it, so he does not make any effort to hide it from Fiona. He tells her he is going down to Harrington's betting office to have a few quid on this outsider, just a bit of fun.

But he has all the holiday cash with him, about €1,000, and in the time between his arrival in Harrington's and the start of the Scottish Grand National, he has lost all but €100 of it, betting in hundreds on horses that keep losing. Instead of having 'a bit of fun' that might throw another €1,000 or two into the holiday funds, he is relying entirely on this outsider in a very long race, with a lot of big fences and dangers of all kinds, to get him out of a very big hole that has opened up so quickly, he hardly has time to feel the fear, to panic – or to figure out what the hell he might say to Fiona, what crazy excuse he could concoct to cover this.

With the little bit of reason that is left to him, he takes the 'conservative' option of having €50 each way on *Run For Paddy*, which at odds as big as this will leave him in the clear if it wins. And even if it doesn't win, but finishes second, third or fourth, he will get back about half his losses.

Run For Paddy finishes first, in a terrifyingly close finish, jockey Carl Llewellyn coming with a late surge to beat the favourite, Ruby Walsh's *Ladalko*, on the line. So it is a huge disappointment for the majority, but a moment of sensational release for Tony 10, which he celebrates not by going home as fast as he can and resolving never to enter a betting office again, but by blowing another few hundred of his winnings in the haze of euphoria, so that eventually he arrives home about €100 to the good. He explains to Fiona that he made this profit by having a fiver each way on *Run For Paddy.*

So even as he is walking slowly into that proverbial tide, there are still these days of victory that seem to pump him full of this powerful anaesthetic, enabling him to forget how far out he is getting, how distant he is now from any reality he once knew.

One of these days is Tuesday, 30 May 2006, his birthday, which he shares with Steven Gerrard. This happy coincidence persuades him to have €800 on Stevie to score first for England in a pre-World Cup friendly against Hungary at Old Trafford. A win would bring a birthday bonus of about five grand.

To bet on a friendly international in the first place is a sure sign of a decline in standards, one that is compounded by the nature of the bet, the 'who-will-score-the-first-goal?' market that the bookies tend to advertise heavily, in the endless quest to lure the mug punter. There is also the superstitious aspect, the shared birthday with Stevie, all of it pointing to a potentially unhappy outcome. And so it is looking after forty-two minutes of the game, when Gerrard is fouled in the box (or dived, if truth be told), the penalty to be taken by Frank Lampard.

That would be 'Lamps' who hardly ever misses a penalty, a fact recognised by Tony as signalling the end of his day's entertainment. Except Lampard misses this one, the keeper saving it with his legs, and the ball rebounds to Michael Owen, who heads it onto the crossbar. Somehow the €800 is still alive, but just before half-time David Beckham swings in a cross for Joe Cole, who heads it against the post, the ball then bouncing along the Hungary goal-line until it is lashed clear by a defender, hitting his own crossbar on the way.

Several miracles have apparently happened to get this game to half-time without some England player other than Stevie getting the first goal. They are just into the second half when a cross from Beckham is headed low into the left-hand corner of the net by one Steven Gerrard. That's five grand in the left-hand corner of the net for Tony 10.

Tony recalls he had a tendency to get a bit full of himself when he had such a win, buying rounds of drinks like a high roller. But one thing he doesn't do that night is have another bet. He manages to sit on that five grand, savouring it, unwilling to risk any let-down on this occasion.

That would come the next day.

It starts on a virtuous note, when he withdraws €2,000 of his Gerrard winnings at 7.00 a.m. That leaves €3,200 in his account, but not for long. There follows a kind of a frenzy of losing on various low-grade races at tracks such as Brighton, Yarmouth and Cartmel, forty-two transactions in all, bets of €200 and €300 and €500 going down all the time, starting around lunchtime and ending at 8.30 p.m. when he switches from the horses to the football to deposit another €1,000, backing Italy to beat Switzerland in a friendly (another friendly) in Geneva. He arrives home after this terrible day at the races, and the match is on Eurosport. He places the bet just before the second half starts, with the score at 1–1. He also has €400 on Alessandro Del Piero to score. Del Piero doesn't, there are no more goals in the game.

His losses for the day amount to nearly €9,000, he wins about €2,500. By late on this Wednesday afternoon he has already gone through the Gerrard profits and is starting to make deposits. He is experiencing these brutal mood swings, between grief and elation, at a rate that is almost unimaginable, and he is doing this while being obliged to carry on as if nothing much is happening at all.

In that thing called ordinary life, he and Fiona are saving up their hard-earned money to pay about ten grand for a wedding in Cyprus. In this other life he is winning and losing thousands on a Wednesday afternoon.

And there's the World Cup coming.

◆ ◆ ◆

While his day-to-day gambling is becoming more compulsive, betting on events just because they are on and because he can't stop himself getting involved, for the World Cup in South Africa he has a plan. A strategy, even. He makes a clinical analysis of the first games in each group, and on the night before the opening game he constructs an accumulator based on the half-time/full-time markets, which means he is backing these teams both to be leading at half-time and to win the game.

He selects Germany, Argentina, England and Holland for this 'acca', which, if it comes up, will return almost ten grand. One notes the presence here of Argentina and Holland, the teams who were involved in that other World Cup bet in 1998, the one that kicked it all off for Tony 10.

In the opening game of the 2006 World Cup tournament, Germany v Costa Rica, the German full-back Lahm scores a cracker after six minutes. Disturbingly enough, Paulo Wanchope equalises for Costa Rica after twelve minutes, but Klose puts Germany ahead again within five minutes, and they hold the lead to half-time. The first part of this epic wager is done, the Germans make it 3–1 on sixty-one minutes, but then the old anxiety strikes again when Wanchope scores another to make it 3–2. Mercifully, Frings gets a fourth, and whatever about the Germans' efforts to win the World Cup in their own country, they have done their bit for Tony 10.

On then to England, playing Paraguay the following afternoon, and 'scoring' after three minutes through an own-goal. That leaves only another forty-two minutes for Tony to endure until half-time, and the whole of the second half, and yet England somehow do it, which means that the second leg of the accumulator is up.

That evening it's Argentina against Ivory Coast, with Crespo and Saviola putting Argentina ahead by half-time, and then surviving a late goal by Didier Drogba for Ivory coast, bringing Tony three-quarters of the way to the promised land.

The next day Holland must be beating Serbia & Montenegro at half-time and full-time. They get the first part done when Arjen Robben scores after eighteen minutes. In fact, they get it all done, because that is how it ends, another game that is close enough to put Tony through many torments, but which ends up with a number in his account that says €9,687.50.

Not only does this kill the pain of any recent defeats, it gives Tony 10 a feeling of vindication, that he can still make a measured assessment of a game of football – of four games of football – and then watch it all happening as he had imagined it would. Moreover, it was just the way he likes it best – a low stake with a high return. At this time he is not much given to the ways of the professional gambler, who will tend to invest very large stakes for a relatively small return, just to give himself less chance of losing. Tony 10 is not going for that method, or at least, not going for it yet.

High on the improbability of this perfectly constructed accumulator, he is off again on the horses, evidently returning to his more compulsive ways, just betting on things because they exist at that moment in time. On 14 July, for example, there are forty-one transactions. Anything else in his life, at work or at home, is on automatic pilot at this point, there is really nothing else in his head but gambling.

While the occasional arrival of five grand or ten grand into the account is stoking up the fever, it is also keeping the domestic finances vaguely manageable – until the time comes in the middle of July when it is all just unmanageable, a situation that calls for an almost guaranteed winner. And while there is no such thing in this world, still there is Tiger Woods.

Tony 10 has €900 on Tiger to win the British Open at Royal Liverpool. This is a bet like the World Cup accumulator, one to which he gives much consideration, given that awful need of his for a substantial win. In which case the greatness of Tiger might just provide the extra ingredient needed to give him the edge.

The night before the Open he can't sleep, the racket in his head just will not stop. He gets out of bed and goes downstairs to use the laptop. At five minutes to three in the morning he has €500 that he really can't afford on Tiger Woods. And then just before 9.00 a.m. he adds another €400, which, at odds of 3/1, would return €3,000 – nowhere near as much as previous winners, but even more important at this particular time.

Tiger does not let him down. He is always prominent, one shot behind the leader after the first round, surging into the lead in round two with a 65, still leading by one from Chris DiMarco, Ernie Els and Sergio García after round three, and holding off the challenge of DiMarco, in particular, to win the Open by two shots.

Tiger's father, Earl Woods, had died in May, making the win all the more emotional for the golfer. And in the back bar of Scraggs Alley in Carlow, Tony 10, for his own reasons, is in a state of some emotion. He and Fiona have gone there to meet friends, but as the last round intensifies at Royal Liverpool, Tony 10 takes himself up to the counter to concentrate on the golf on the pub television.

Indeed, such is his need for Tiger to get it done, it draws a curious remark from Fiona. 'You have a big interest in this.' Something in his demeanour is making her uneasy. But he manages to dismiss it and compose himself again.

This is the first time that he lets it slip, that he forgets for a moment to maintain the proverbial poker face. But he avoids any further discovery because Tiger, after all, has done the business for him. Released once more from the worst of all prospects – the prospect that he might have to stop gambling – Tony 10 is tranquilised again, still unaware that he might be that guy in the cartoon image, slowly walking into the sea.

Nor is he conscious at this stage that in the light of what is yet to come, the water is only up to his knees.

CHAPTER 10

By winning the Epsom Derby on 2 June 2007, *Authorised*, trained by Peter Chapple-Hyam and ridden by Frankie Dettori, paid for Tony 10's wedding to Fiona. Not that she had any awareness of this fact, and not that any of the approximately eighty friends and relations who had gone with them to Cyprus had any awareness of it.

It gives us a sense of Tony O'Reilly's standing in the community and with his extended family that eighty people would make this journey to celebrate with him. He had been at the centre of things for so long in Scraggs and with the football team and generally knocking around the town of Carlow, not only has he no difficulty rounding up that wedding party, there are a few extra revellers at the airport he had hardly expected to be there at all.

But though they all know him well, or think they do, only he knows that there are more things weighing on the mind of Tony 10 than have ever troubled Tony O'Reilly. The last instalment of the payment to the hotel for the wedding – about five grand – still has to be paid. And he has the money to pay it, on his MBNA credit card. He has just about managed to keep it there without using it for gambling, and since he is going to a place where logistically he will not be able to gamble in his usual way – he isn't bringing his laptop – he is happy as he leaves Dublin that there will be no problem about settling this particular bill. He does not know how much of his happiness will be depending on events still to take place,

not in some hotel in the Aegean, but at the new Wembley
Stadium and at Epsom Downs.

Authorised is the last leg of a four-way accumulator that
had started on 26 May when *Artimino* won a competitive
handicap at Newmarket at odds of 9/2. Then, on 27 May,
Seville beat Real Zaragoza 3–1 at home, which means that as
the wedding party is leaving Dublin airport the following day,
the groom is aware that he is almost halfway towards a very
nice wedding present of about five grand from Paddy Power.
Not that he desperately needs that extra money on this trip,
but it would still be most acceptable – for this accumulator to
click, he still needs Derby County to gain promotion to the
Premier League in the play-off final at Wembley on 28 May,
and finally he needs *Authorised* to win the Derby.

It is a remarkable aspect of this story, and one that is
coming unprompted from the man himself, that by the
middle of 2007 even an occasion as supposedly important
as his wedding has come to be inextricably linked with the
challenges it is presenting to him as a gambler.

And yet as he leaves Dublin he feels that he is taking a
kind of holiday from his obsession. It is not unknown even
for compulsive gamblers to feel like this when they find
themselves in strange surroundings, seeing it as a chance
perhaps to switch off the engines for a while, all the better
to get them going again on their return. That accumulator
aside, Tony is really trying to participate in these wedding
arrangements, to avoid reaching the familiar cut-off point at
which Fiona is just not there anymore, because he is unable to
pay much attention to any living thing other than the horses
and the footballers and the golfers and the tennis players who
are representing his interests in the betting arena.

So as they head for Paphos, in Cyprus, to the four-star
Alexander the Great Beach Hotel, for a while it is mainly the

wedding that is on his mind, in this atmosphere of celebration which at times reaches such heights there are people in Carlow who will still say it was the best holiday they ever had.

On the afternoon of their arrival, he and a few friends are able to get a seat in the hotel bar to watch Derby County beating West Bromwich Albion 1–0, the only goal coming on the sixty-first minute, not an easy thing to be watching, on the whole, for a man in Tony 10's situation. Because now the old betting juices are starting to flow again, he has three legs of the four-part accumulator up, so if the favourite *Authorised* wins the Derby, which is being run in four days time, he will be looking at that substantial payout from his online betting provider. Yes the juices are starting to flow again, because he is so optimistic about *Authorised*, he is starting to see that five grand almost as money in the bank. Now he would like to be betting on the strength of that, the way he does at home on the laptop and in the offices, but still he must make do with this accumulator that he put together before the trip – the iPhone which would connect him straight away to his online account had not yet been created in its most miraculous form. So in the hotel bar, he and members of his party are having a few small bets on that play-off final, and such is the release of getting up the third leg of the accumulator, Tony 10 hardly notices the relatively small amounts of cash he is winning from friends. He has much more riding on this.

In the meantime, there is this business of getting married. The day itself has been shifted from 29 May, so that it will now be on 30 May, a delay caused by the collapse of the XL airline on which Fiona's family had been booked to travel. But this crisis has an upside too, a bad omen balanced out by a good one, because 30 May is Tony 10's birthday. And he would clearly be enjoying this happy coincidence of his birthday and his wedding even more if part of his mind was not on that other galaxy, in which the fourth leg of a substantial accumulator is pending.

Then a new permutation arrives into play. As Tony 10 is getting accustomed to the hotel facilities, he finds that there is a computer in the lobby – an important discovery at a time when the gambler still occasionally needed access to something as traditional as a computer, especially on a trip to Cyprus. This computer is to him a beautiful sight. Using a Cypriot pound note to buy time online, he quickly establishes that it will enable him to log-on to his Paddy Power account. And with the addiction roaring inside him again, he has a decision to make. The sort of decision which to some extent he had already made in the depths of his being when the third leg of the accumulator came up, a decision that is now ready to be executed.

He starts betting.

Using the money on his MBNA card he starts betting – the money that is supposed to pay for his wedding, but that he now finds irresistible as a source of gambling funds because after all, *Authorised* is going to win the Derby, right? He is virtually home and hosed, right?

Tony 10 starts betting with the wedding money, and he starts losing.

And then he starts winning, but not enough to make up for the losing. He is chipping away, losing and winning and losing again on all the usual markets, the horses and the football and the tennis, and various combinations thereof. He realises early on that he is chasing, that the way it's going, the hole keeps getting deeper no matter how hard he tries to fill it in, to get back to where he started.

He is chiselling away at the money in Cyprus, just like he does back home, until he has little more than 'walking around money' left, until it's really all about *Authorised* again, until his last best hope is the favourite running in the Derby in a few days' time. Except now, with the rest of the money so diminished, the horse doesn't seem to him like such a favourite. Now he is having all sorts of doubts.

Now he is in a place beyond torment, having tried to free himself from all the anxiety for a couple of weeks at least here in Cyprus, only to be dragged right back into it because he just couldn't stop. It's just not in him now to walk away, not for a week, not even for a day if he can manage it.

This time, though, he is so demoralised, so crushed by this latest defeat on the hotel computer, he can't bring himself to risk another bet, can't face the prospect of maxing out the card completely, until *Authorised* has done whatever *Authorised* is going to do. At which point he will either be saved again, or in all likelihood the scale of his addiction will be exposed, he will be found out here, on the occasion of his own wedding.

So each day he and Fiona take the ten-minute walk from the Alexander the Great to the resort where everyone else is staying, most of them lounging by the pool. Indeed, there were four young men from Carlow who drank a lot of Jack Daniel's and headed straight to the pool, where they continued to drink and to engage in watersports for the day, disregarding any advice about the need for sun-screen. They were burned so badly, their blisters were still bursting at the wedding ceremony.

For Tony and Fiona there is the official signing of the documents in the Town Hall, and then it is the night before the church service, which they spend apart for superstitious reasons. Tony stays in the apartment of his best man, Niall.

They have warned the hotel that there will probably be tremendous pressure on the bar throughout the day, and to be sure to have enough staff to cope. But somehow the message doesn't get through, so there is a period during the reception when a kind of panic sets in among the wedding party, when drinks are being brought to tables far too slowly by the standards of the Irish, even allowing for the fact that each table has been supplied with several bottles of wine.

He is not sure if this is what caused him to react as he did, or whether it was his dependence on *Authorised* to pay for all this, but Tony spends a fair while berating the manager for this display of negligence and incompetence. Which is untypical of Tony, but perhaps an indicator of the pressures he is suffering, not just to ensure that everyone is having a good time but that he can foot the bill for it.

The dispute with the management over the drink goes on for so long, he misses most of the excellent band he had hired, and later in the evening, unhappy with the music, he takes to dee-jaying himself. Fiona would describe the reception as the Tony Show, such was his apparent desire for the event to conform with some ideal image in his own head, to take personal responsibility for the success of the night. She does not know what fears are driving the Tony Show. She does not know his appalling need for some sort of release from the hole he has been so assiduously digging for himself.

He has been following *Authorised* for some time, an increasingly unusual practice, consumed as he is these days by the instant reactions of the online punter, to just betting compulsively on whatever appears on the screen in front of him. This explains his descent into the darkness of betting on things he couldn't possibly know anything about, things like under-19 Internationals and the Arsenal Ladies and dodgy tennis matches in Budapest.

Authorised, by contrast, feels like a solid investment, a measured decision. And if there wasn't so much depending on it, he would be quite relaxed about the colt's chances, he would be confidently expecting it to win.

But he is not in any way relaxed. Two days after the reception, now a married man, he sits on the bed in the hotel room watching the race. The Derby is always a very tough one for the punter because Epsom is such an idiosyncratic track. A horse may just not perform on it for reasons that are only evident after the event. There is the fact that Frankie Dettori has never ridden the winner of this race, which is also worrying Tony 10, wondering if for some perverse reason the gods will not allow this to happen. And there are two horses in the race, *Soldier of Fortune* and *Eagle Mountain*, trained by Aidan O'Brien, who is winning such races as if by right.

For Tony 10 there is a little spasm of the deepest fear in the early stages, when *Authorised*, in the green jacket, appears to be struggling to find a position. But as the race develops he is running unhindered, and with three furlongs to go Dettori has him just behind the leaders, a place from which he can win if he is good enough.

Now is the moment in which everything is suspended in the way that is so familiar to Tony 10, those few seconds in which the man who loves things to be in order must give all that away, surrendering it to forces that are utterly beyond his control. Now is the moment at which *Authorised* will either keep running at the same pace and start to drop backwards, or will find something that the others do not have and surge forward.

Authorised finds it. Dettori gives him the signal and he accelerates, a glorious sight as he takes the lead and just keeps going away from the field, winning the race by one of the biggest margins in its history. A glorious sight indeed for a man sitting on a hotel bed in Paphos, exulting in the commentator's line about Dettori's 'date with destiny', as *Authorised* charges towards the finishing line, a certain winner at the furlong pole. It is not just the destiny of Frankie Dettori that is being decided in these moments, and the commentator gets it right with his words after the race – 'just sublime'.

Tony 10 is not only able to pay for his wedding, he is able to treat another couple on the periphery of the wedding party to dinner, telling Fiona he won a few extra hundred from the lads in the bar on Derby County. He tells her nothing about the €4,950 that will be arriving into his account in a couple of days' time, after the Derby – an echo here of the '€800' he declared to Fiona when he had actually won nearly five grand on that seminal double featuring Bobby Zamora and CSKA Moscow.

And of course he will also be able to bet freely on the computer in the lobby with anything that might be left.

◆ ◆ ◆

Over the next few days, as the wedding party starts to break up, leaving just himself and Fiona there for the second week of the holiday, Tony 10 is on a downer.

It goes like this for him, he throws himself completely into something, he builds it all up until he gets the desired result, and then he has this strange feeling of being bereft – what happens now?

It has become a pattern in his work life, in his married life, and every day of the week in his gambling life.

What now?

◆ ◆ ◆

Still, he is becoming convinced that no matter how bad things get, he will always find a way out. That he has, of necessity, become so adept at this crazy juggling, he will always stay in the game somehow. With his natural gifts for organisation and for presentation and for getting on with people, he can do it.

He is thinking that he could have resolved the crisis around the wedding, even if *Authorised* hadn't won, that he is now such a master of scheming he could have juggled that one too. That the urgency to win the bet was mainly about saving face, but that if it hadn't turned out like that on Derby day, he would have sorted it out anyway. And he is probably not wrong about this. He is a very bright and resourceful man, and not only does he win sometimes, he wins big sometimes.

In the months after Cyprus, however, the numbers are telling a different tale. Those raw figures are saying that the money is seeping inexorably from his account into that of Paddy Power, hundreds and hundreds and hundreds going out every day, and not enough of them coming back, until by the middle of August he has maxed out his credit card and can't find a way to borrow any more money.

At that time you couldn't lodge money to your Paddy Power online account over the counter in the betting office – that facility would not be available until February 2010. He has been topping up his various bank and credit union loans to such an extent, he can't top them up any more, or at least he will have to wait for some decent interval to elapse before trying again. It is now the second half of 2007, perhaps the financial institutions that had been virtually forcing money on their customers are starting to sense that something isn't quite right with their game either, that their gambling is getting out of control.

The last bet of Tony 10 before going offline for a while is €100 on a nine-part accumulator featuring Aberdeen, Arsenal, Chelsea, Dundalk, Kilmarnock, Manchester United, Shelbourne, Torquay and Tottenham, a hugely unlikely proposition that displays his desperation for just one enormous victory that might keep the online show going for another while.

The bet goes down.

For the rest of 2007 his gambling needs are met by cash bets in the office and poker games in pubs – actual games with other human beings, using 'real' money.

He struggles through until the new year and a transfusion of money he manages to extract from the credit union, another five grand. This gets him back online again, though the bet that he remembers most keenly from this period is a cash accumulator he had in a betting office in Castledermot.

He would go through Castledermot, about seven miles outside Carlow, on his way home from the Greystones post office where he spent the odd day training junior employees in counter procedures and about the job in general. He was often sent to train people in other branches too, including the one in Gorey, a reminder of how highly Tony O'Reilly was regarded within the organisation.

But Tony 10 also has work to do, such as this €50 accumulator he has in May 2008 on a few horses and football matches, six events in all, the last of which is Chelsea to beat Manchester United in the final of the Champions League in Moscow.

He had a shattering experience in the semi-final, when John Arne Riise of Liverpool scored an own-goal in the last minute against Chelsea, which hadn't cost Tony 10 a lot of money – at this stage €700 isn't much – but which had sent him straight to bed literally to cover his head, with a feeling of black depression due to the fact that he also had the emotional involvement of a Liverpool diehard. So to be waiting on Chelsea to win the final seems to promise a kind of redemption.

It is a Friday evening when he drops into the little privately owned office in Castledermot to have his bet. The racing is on, and a couple of his horses win. But there is still the football to come at the weekend, which duly clicks up a few more legs of the accumulator, leaving a few days until the final, which is now worth €12,000 to Tony 10, that is, if Chelsea can do it. He needs that money, he needs it so badly, he has a visceral craving for it and the relief it would bring.

For the owner of the office in Castledermot, that €12,000 payout might just be enough to close him down. So he is feeling the fear too, that this guy he vaguely recognises, who just drops in one evening with his €50 bastard accumulator, is going to ruin his life.

Everyone with an interest in the game remembers one thing above all else about that final, that John Terry slips as he is taking his penalty in the shoot-out, the ball skimming the outside of the post and winning the Champions League for United. Such a cruel outcome for Terry, and for Chelsea.

Such a cruel outcome for Tony 10, shattered as he watches John Terry sitting on the sodden pitch with his head bowed between his knees, while the keeper van der Sar celebrates. And at that precise moment, for the bookie in Castledermot there is salvation.

CHAPTER 11

One more time Tony goes back to the bank, one more time, in mid-2008, he squeezes another €5,000 out of a legitimate lender using words like 'home improvements'. One more time it all goes down the Swanee, this time more quickly than usual, because he is offline again within a fortnight, just failing again and again to click the one accumulator that will make everything all right.

The global crash is gripping the country now, and it will be harder to get money for anything. For Tony 10 the only 'consolation' is that he has found a new way to pursue his obsession. Just as he is running out of money again in his Sports Betting account, he notes that a free bet of €200 is waiting in his Casino account, a thoughtful gesture from his online betting provider, through which he discovers the pleasures of online poker.

Using this free bet, he wins straightaway in a game of Texas Hold 'Em, and then transfers his winnings to his Sports section, punting that few hundred up and down in the more familiar manner, until he is back to zero again. Yet this brief exposure gives him a taste for the Casino side of things, for the pure escapism of staying up half the night playing poker because he can't sleep, a form of the compulsion that will return to him at a later stage, when he has more resources available to him.

For now, though, he is an addict without the means to fill that great emptiness. It is so ingrained in him, he is like one of those racing experts who can 'price' the horses independently of the bookie. He can take a look at most sporting propositions and work out what the odds on each contender should be. He has the fever. But he just doesn't have the money to get involved to a meaningful degree, and not at all online. He has so many loans and so much juggling to do in that regard, there is no way he can support the covert activities of Tony 10.

Tony O'Reilly of An Post, on the other hand, is doing very well. In June 2009 he goes for an interview for a further promotion from his current status as Acting Branch Manager in Carlow, to the position of Branch Manager in Gorey. It is a job for which there are many candidates, who arrive on this day to the grand premises of the Heritage Hotel in Laois.

Tony gives a presentation to the interview panel, with a particular emphasis on marketing and customer service, feeling that this will give him an edge over the other applicants, who happen to include two hopefuls from the Gorey branch itself. His references are also excellent, with much praise for the meticulous nature of his work and his charismatic personality, which is demonstrated on the day when he sits down in front of the panel and nearly falls off the swivel chair. He immediately gathers himself and turns it into a joke, which lightens the atmosphere for all in the room.

He gets the job.

At a time when large numbers of people in Ireland are being destroyed by the recession, here is Tony O'Reilly moving up all the time, permanent and pensionable, only in his mid-thirties and about to become one of the youngest branch managers in the country. He even has a plan beyond this, because he is aware that the present manager in Carlow is not far off retirement. Ideally, he will assume that role when the time comes.

All he needs now is a car that will bring him every day from Carlow to work in Gorey. He can't cycle there, and he knows he will have serious difficulty getting a loan for a new car because of all the other loans out there already. Tony 10 has managed to bring about a situation whereby Tony O'Reilly may not be able to accept this promotion, because he can't afford to buy a car – and because he clearly can't admit to anyone the reason why a man who is having such apparent success in his life can't afford to buy a car.

There are no public transport options between Carlow and Gorey, so he will need a car. His only hope is to make one last grovelling approach to the credit union, using two things which are to his advantage – the fact that he is about to get an excellent and secure job and a raise, and the fact that he is driven by a ferocious desire to conceal the nature of his addiction.

He gets the loan. He gets what he needs for the car, and a bit more than what he needs, for gambling. Maybe he is right, maybe he will always find a way.

Gorey has for long been known as 'a good town', with a busy air about it. That part of Co. Wexford has a long tradition of attracting visitors to the beaches for the day or to their mobile homes along the coast, and Gorey benefits from all this. It is also just within the limit of being an acceptable commuting distance from Dublin. The long main street is dominated at one end by a hill, on which there is a junction feared by many of the learner drivers who come to Gorey to do their driving test. The various narrow side streets and the complex flow of traffic down the town leading out to the motorway are thought to be ideal for interrogating the skills of the provisional licence holder.

To get to the post office, you can drive up the main street, through the two sets of traffic lights and, when you get to the junction on the hill, turn left into The Avenue. It is one of the older types of post office, a substantial single-storey, redbrick building, which has been there since the start of the twentieth century. And while its old walls have seen much, in all likelihood they have not seen anything like the events that were about to unfold with the arrival of the new branch manager.

It is not an easy start for Tony. He feels there is a certain resentment towards him not just because he is a 'moderniser' but because it is felt in the office that the job should have gone to someone who was working there already. Tony accepts that these are not unreasonable complaints, and that it's up to him to win people over, a task that might seem more manageable if it wasn't for all the other things he has to win too.

Just before he is due to take up the new job, he and Fiona learn that she is pregnant. That is wonderful news in most ways, except one – when she eventually has to go on maternity leave, there will be less money, and Tony 10 alone knows how little of that there is already. He is getting former colleagues to hold his post, so that he can keep bank statements away from his door where Fiona might find them. He is shredding all credit card statements.

So disengaged has he become from the better parts of life that even this happiest of days, when he learns he is going to be a father, is soon darkened by the fear – how is he going to manage? It feels like he is living through a kind of constant panic attack, the root cause of which is the gambling, but the only medication for which is also the gambling, or so it seems to him.

In these early days in Gorey, he is getting that medication, and a few successes, at the betting office nearest to the post office. In fact, he believes he was partly responsible for closing it down. He had clicked a few accumulators, betting in cash across the counter, winning a couple of grand a few times. His biggest win amounted to €6,000, at which point the woman behind the counter said that she couldn't take any more of his bets. She put it plainly: 'You're winning too much.'

It was a stance that proved to be self-defeating, not just because it deprived the bookie of the opportunity of getting it all back, as so often happens in such situations, but because other punters, including some of Tony's new colleagues in the post office, took umbrage at this attitude and boycotted the office, which closed soon afterwards. A moral victory, of sorts, for Tony 10.

But there are other betting offices in Gorey, where he is not winning. There are branches of BoyleSports, Ladbrokes and Paddy Power within a few hundred yards of the post office, and he is in them every day, leaving a lot more money behind than he is taking out. Soon, he is also able to lodge cash across the counter to his Paddy Power online account.

All the while he is trying to get back to some mythical place before he started gambling, all the while he is looking for that colossal accumulator that will undo all the damage and allow him to pay off his credit card and his loans and to get out of this deepening hole. But the accumulators, by their nature, also have this quality of keeping him absorbed in multiple bets throughout the day. They serve his addiction even as they seem to promise a way out of it.

Still, in these early days in Gorey, he does manage to motivate the staff who might have resented him at first. He turns around the offices in a few months to such an extent, when An Post runs what it calls a Customer Plus scheme, the Gorey branch is rated the seventh best in the country. It is one of the more puzzling aspects of addiction for those who are not involved, that a person can declare themselves an alcoholic or a compulsive gambler even though it had seemed that they were working to a very high standard. Yet there is a simple logic to it: the overwhelming need to keep achieving at a certain level so that the addiction can be maintained and disguised.

However, the better that Tony O'Reilly does, the more it seems that Tony 10 is determined to take the good out of it.

The economic crash has benefitted An Post in an odd way. People are now so distrustful of banks, they are more inclined to put their money in the post office, which is State guaranteed. And whereas once they would have had to discuss their investments at the counter, Tony sets up a section where they can organise these matters in private. Within a few months he re-energises the place, transforming it from something out of the 1950s into a progressive establishment, and yet almost from the start he is struggling even to pay for petrol to put in the car to get him there and back.

In fact, in January 2010, when the bills and the gambling wipe out his wages in a day, he actually doesn't have the money to get home from the office. He takes an 'increment' of €600, which he is not supposed to do, without clearance. For this he receives a visit from the Operations Manager, who gives him a severe warning, which is lucky because, in theory, he could have been sacked for this. Perhaps if his performance since his arrival in Gorey hadn't been otherwise exemplary, he would have been sacked.

Tony was expecting the reprimand, but he is still shocked at how close he has come to losing his career. He admits to the Operations Manager that he is struggling financially. He talks about the usual pressures of the mortgage and of starting a family, he mutters excuses about being paid fortnightly and how he has to adjust his finances to that. He doesn't mention that he is starting to see no way out of this, no way at all, except to start taking money. That any 'increments' he might be taking from now on will be strictly off the record.

CHAPTER 12

I t starts with the bags of coins.

In the haven of his office, branch manager Tony O'Reilly takes two €2 bags out of a clear coin delivery bag, each of the €2 bags containing €50 in all. Then he re-seals the delivery bag with tape, marking the bag with a marker so he will know this is a bag that is short.

The first time he takes €100, exchanging the €2 bags within the branch for notes. He will eventually take €2,000 in this way before moving on to the bundles of notes.

Tony 10 is far enough gone at this stage to regard this as the inevitable form of the scheming to which he has become accustomed, this incessant robbing Peter to pay Paul. Except up to this, he wasn't actually robbing Peter as such, he was just borrowing from him with an increasingly small chance of being able to pay him back. Now he is literally robbing, and using all the ingenuity he has developed to cover it up. He is discovering that, like all the loans from the bank and the credit union, €2,000 will never be enough. He will need far more serious amounts of money, the kind that you can't get in €50 bags of coins.

So he moves on to the notes. Again, there is ingenuity in it, as there has to be. The bundles of €50,000 in €50 notes are coming either in plastic wrapping or with a tape around them. He prefers the ones with the tape because the notes in them are more tightly packed, which means the bundle is still tight if he takes out a few of the notes – which he does, using a blue pliers. Later he finds a small black knife with an extremely sharp blade that also does the job.

He is taking €2,000 at a time, as if the grand total of €2,000 from the coins was just a rehearsal for this, a reflection of the way his betting shot up from the tens to the hundreds to the thousands.

He remembers a moment around this time when he's in the car with Niall Byrne, talking about life in general and nothing in particular, and he has this enormous urge to tell Niall how bad things have become, the extent of his gambling, the whole thing.

He has this opportunity, after giving Niall a lift home, sitting outside his house late at night, to tell at least this one person the truth. He knows he can trust Niall completely with any information. He is finding the stress of keeping all this to himself unbearable, and yet he can't bring himself to say the words, even to Niall. He just bottles it.

He looks back on this now with a feeling of infinite sadness, but also with a sense that for a gambler at that stage of the game, such moments will always come, and they will always go. There is no rock bottom, it seems, when somewhere in the depths of your psyche you still feel there's this possibility of turning it all around. It is so hard to say 'it's over' when there is always this inner voice telling you that somehow it might not be over yet. That everything might still be all right.

There's a day in Gorey too, just before he starts taking the money, when he is having lunch with his father, Tony Senior, in the '62' café. They discuss various financial difficulties of the ordinary kind that he is having, the way that he is struggling to pay back loans, the shortage of cash in general. He suggests to his father that a solution might be found whereby Tony Senior would advance him his share of the family home, which would mean that repayments would be made by Tony Junior to his father rather than to some inflexible institution. And yes, he really would make these repayments, he still believes he can turn it all around.

He can talk freely to his father about these things because Tony Senior is a bright and capable man who would be open to finding such a solution, if it seemed to make sense. Indeed, if Tony Junior had done what he desperately wanted to do during that meeting and had told his father the real reason for his financial troubles, in all likelihood, after the shock had landed and the realities become apparent, he would have received some very practical help. In all likelihood he would have avoided a mountain of grief.

He would not have received any financial help, indeed his father is adamant that he would not have bailed out Tony if he'd known that his financial struggles were down to gambling. But he would have received the kind of help he really needed, for this addiction which is dominating his days.

Again the fear gets the better of him, and he does not do what he desperately wants to do. His pride is destroying him, his ego will not allow him to let go of his secret, it will stay locked inside of him, consuming him. And his ideas for re-engineering the family's financial structures will also drift away, because soon he will be making more elaborate arrangements.

None of the fear that visits him most days is drifting away. Always he is conscious that there are An Post audits to be passed, the first of which is due around April or May. So while he is performing these illicit operations to physically remove the cash from the bundles and to take it with him to the office of Paddy Power and sometimes to BoyleSports and Ladbrokes, he is also falsifying the figures by making 'fictitious' lodgements to the cash safe, using his position as the person in charge to alter the numbers in the Accountable Receipts.

At one level he is being clever, using all his knowledge of the system to take money without anyone noticing. At another level, one of black farce, he sometimes sees himself as the Jim Carrey character in *Dumb and Dumber*, Lloyd Christmas, who replaces cash with IOUs as if there's a hope in hell that he'll be able to turn those ridiculous scraps of paper back into real money.

On the day of the first audit he is feeling some of the fear, but then he is so accustomed to awaiting the results of other potentially life-ruining events it is almost becoming a normal state of being. Looking at it objectively, he reckons he has covered up his activities well enough to get through this audit, which is not the most stringent of the tests that he must face.

And sure enough, he passes it. He has tea and scones in a nearby restaurant with the auditor, who has no idea at all that when his lunch companion is alone in his office, he has a method of surgically removing €50 notes from a bundle, a method he is honing to a kind of art-form.

But in this game Tony 10 is playing, there is never an end, there is always some other crazy obstacle to be negotiated. There will be another audit two weeks from now, on a bigger scale. And for this, calculating what he has taken from the sealed bundles of notes, he figures that he will be €8,000 short. He would have no problem at all if he had won the €12,000 that was coming to him from a couple of accas he had in BoyleSports, both of which were depending on the result of one tennis match, in which his player was leading 3–0 in the final set. And managed to lose it from there.

So he is €8,000 down, and yet he still believes that he will probably pass the audit, because he is getting more confident in his machinations, and because in a town the size of Gorey large amounts of money are coming in and out of the post office to cover pensions and disability and social welfare payments and savings, so this €8,000 probably won't be too hard to conceal. And he knows that usually they don't check bundles of notes that seem secure, only the loose ones. Yes, he figures he should get away with this discrepancy of €8,000, but he'd like to make sure of that.

It comes to him as he is driving home, on that road he takes every evening with his mind racing at a thousand miles an hour, through the towns of Shillelagh or Hacketstown or Tullow or Castledermot and their betting offices. There is, he realises, just one person to whom he can go, to ask for that €8,000.

He drives to Carlow, to ask Colette, his mother, for the money. And while it is easier at a certain level to ask for this loan than to be dealing with an uncaring institution, there is also a more profound risk to it. He feels that his mother has always regarded him as the blue-eyed boy, that she had been disappointed in him during his earlier escapades, such as throwing away the chance of a sound job in the sugar factory and then dropping out of college after a year. Now that he is doing so well, on the face of it, and feels he has redeemed himself in her eyes, he most certainly doesn't want to lay on her the much more savage disappointment she would undoubtedly feel if this gambling business were to turn seriously ugly.

But he really needs that eight grand. And he seriously believes that he will be able to give it all back to her. He is as sure of this as he can be of anything. At his parents' home, he explains to Colette that with Fiona going on maternity leave, and so on and so forth, everything is going to be a bit tricky for a while, but this is just a temporary problem, more of a cash-flow issue than anything else.

Colette agrees to give him the money, she has no reason to imagine that anything else could be wrong. She arranges with her credit union for a cheque to be issued for that amount, and Tony assures her that he will pay her back on a weekly basis. At that moment he means it, too, even if it adds yet another repayment to the many he already has to make.

On this occasion, however, the scheming of Tony 10 goes somewhat awry. He has made a miscalculation.

He had vacillated about asking his mother for the money before finally doing so, and it takes time for credit union procedures to be completed. As a result, on the day he is sitting down with the audit team in Gorey, he has a cheque for €8,000 in his pocket which he hasn't yet been able to lodge to the credit of An Post.

Again, the atmosphere is quite cordial – Tony will go for lunch with them – but there is no doubting the seriousness of the team. There are two of them with him in his office, going through everything, and another three in the rest of the building, checking all the things that a post office auditor is supposed to check. When all this detailed checking is finished they find … nothing.

He knew that he was getting good at this, but he ends the day with a feeling of near invincibility. His head is already busy, thinking of that €8,000 that is now available to him. It seems that having proved his abilities at every other aspect of the job, he is reserving some of his finest performances for these heart-stopping episodes of fraud and falsification.

So now he has that €8,000, and of course part of him knows that the only thing to do now is to give it back to his mother, with thanks. But the other part of him, which is now the dominant part, can think only of this €8,000 as ammunition that might enable him to get back to that better place he left a long time ago. A place in which he never has to do this sort of thing again.

This is how he justifies the fact that he is now, essentially, stealing from his own mother.

◆ ◆ ◆

It is up to nineteen or twenty hours a day now, the gambling is utterly consuming him. He is becoming isolated in his own home, spending much of his time in the kitchen on the laptop, while Fiona is in the sitting room. He is becoming isolated even when he is in the same room as Fiona, who might be watching television while he is gazing into the laptop on his knee, betting thousands in the course of the evening. If Fiona asks what he is doing, he says he is following the football or some other sport, a plausible enough explanation since she is well aware of his love of sports. What she is not aware of is the thousands that he is making or losing right there on the couch, on the screen that he can see but that is hidden from her. When he can't find some form of sport to keep him involved, he is getting into the casino games on Paddy Power online, that €200 free bet they gave him proving a most astute investment on their part.

He is betting for much of the day, and he is stopping in betting offices on his way home from work. He is betting long into the night.

Now there are bundles of €5,000, which he wraps with an elastic band, ready for the day's punting. In his postmaster's office he has betting dockets from Paddy Power on which he writes his selections, usually two or three accumulators, for a grand or two grand each. He takes these down to the betting office on the main street, about 200 yards away if he uses the back gate of the post office. And when he gets there, usually he will wait for a quiet moment before handing the bundle swiftly to the person behind the counter. They will take it from him without counting it, knowing the routine.

Later in the day he may need to pass another €5,000 and another docket across the counter in this literally underhanded way, but if his accumulator is successful, they will add the winnings to the balance in his online account. Usually in that case he will add a tip of €100 or €200 for the person behind the counter.

Even as he is wrapping yet another elastic band around another five grand, he does not contemplate the idea of using one of these bundles to pay off some of the loans he has taken out from banks or credit unions, though he is on his way towards owing about €50,000 to such institutions. He can't bear to 'waste' any of this precious money. He has lost all interest in buying things in general. He wants only to buy time in the gambling zone.

It is now about the middle of 2010. With the baby due in August, whatever joy it brings him is being sabotaged by this overwhelming anxiety. He is, in theory, married to Fiona and about to become a father, but emotionally and physically he is exhausted, removing himself from all such normality. He finds that the unending stress is bringing on bouts of dry-retching, which reaches an apogee one morning as a scene materialises whereby Fiona is in one bathroom, vomiting due to morning sickness, while in the other bathroom he is retching.

Yet there is some strange energy in the addiction of gambling which also enables him to maintain that front, to give nothing away, to endure these moments of ecstasy and of grief in this state of profound silence, always thinking that he is so close to making everything all right. Thinking of the ones that just got away from him – John Terry only missed that penalty due to a freak occurrence, after all, like John Arne

Riise's own-goal in the last minute, it was just an appalling accident. Tony 10 had essentially made the right calls there, he had made a lot of right calls, and now he just needs the ball to break in his direction. Maybe just once.

By August he is still losing. He is taking more and more money from the post office to feed the obsession. As he awaits the birth of his child, he figures that he has taken more than €60,000 from An Post. And he figures that the only possible way he can find that €60,000 is by taking more money from the same place, and gambling with it.

◆ ◆ ◆

On the night of 28 August 2010, he is in Ardkeen Hospital in Waterford. It is turning out to be a long labour for Fiona, a long time too for Tony 10, who tries to shorten the journey somewhat on his smartphone with a five-part football acca and a bet on a horse. This will result in a combined loss of a relatively trivial €700. The betting corporations are careful not to portray such images of distracted fatherhood in their TV advertising.

As Fiona's labour continues through the following day, he finds his fortunes improving. He is advised by members of the Ardkeen staff to head off into the city for a coffee. He takes this to mean a trip to the nearest betting office, which happens to be a branch of BoyleSports. Betting on the horses and the dogs, he takes about two grand out of the bookie's satchel, which would be a big thrill for most people, a sign that this really was their lucky day, what with the imminent arrival of the child along with this gift from the gods.

For Tony 10, it's not quite the same. It's a decent enough return, of course, but in another way it just reminds him of how far he has to go, how even the good days are tinged with melancholia.

After twenty-four hours in labour, Fiona gives birth to their daughter, Hailey. It is 2.00 a.m. and Tony 10 is in the waiting room, looking across the car park, and he is thinking that he is going to lose everything. All this euphoria at the birth of Hailey is being ruined by thoughts of what is to come.

He wants to go in there and express all sorts of love and admiration for Fiona, for the baby, but he has this weight pressing down on him. He finds it unbearable to think that Fiona, and this baby that she wanted so much, may have this terrible thing coming to them. That he is bringing this trouble into Fiona's life, into Hailey's life, into his own life, or at least into whatever part of it he has not yet already squandered.

In the first picture of the two of them together, he doesn't look like a man would usually look in those hours just after he has become a father for the first time. There is no joy or excitement or relief in his expression. It does not appear to be a scene of celebration. He is not even smiling. He just looks wasted.

He is on two weeks' paternity leave from work, he is down that €60,000, there will be another major audit, probably in December, and in the meantime he can only hope to God that the measures he has taken to conceal the missing €60,000 will work. He has told the person deputising for him in this area that there is about €60,000 in coin in a safe, which she will not be able to check because he has hidden the key. So when she balances at the end of Wednesday, she will add this fictitious €60,000 and hopefully life will go on.

But as he sits in the hospital waiting room in the quiet of the early hours, he can't see it going on for much longer. He is going to lose all this, for sure. He has just become a father, he should be looking forward to all sorts of great things, yet here he is, looking across this car park, and it is all shot through with this awful sadness. He feels utterly alone.

At this stage, €60,000 down, how can he possibly even think of telling Fiona about it? She is in there, consumed with all that this new life is promising, consumed in the right way. Is he supposed to find a way to break this to her, to inform her that they are not, in fact, embarking on some exciting new part of their lives, that it may all be ending very badly, very soon?

No, he can't possibly do that. But the alternative is equally heartbreaking, to see her on this night of all nights, so unaware of what is coming down the line. To see Hailey, so unaware of this madness that she will eventually hear about, that she will have to deal with in her own way. And even if he could tell Fiona, tell anyone, he feels that it is too late now. That sixty grand might as well be sixty million, the damage is done, the only way out of this that is even vaguely imaginable to him is just to keep betting, to keep hoping.

He sees some other man who has just become a father walking across the car park and getting into his car and driving away. He would love to be that man, he would love to be anyone but who he is right now.

◆ ◆ ◆

When he returns to Gorey in September, having dodged the bullet again, that number, €60,000, which was already terrifying, is shooting up to six figures. It's all €1,000s, €1,500s, €2,000s that he's staking now, on singles, doubles, accumulators, casino games. That number will eventually reach nearly €300,000 by Christmas, when that audit is due.

He is slipping the bundles of 5,000 across the counter of the betting office at an even faster rate, the first one when he arrives in the office in the morning and another on his way out, maybe twenty minutes later, the same again later in the day, the operation now honed to a kind of crazy perfection.

And yet … if a game in the Belgian Cup in late October had finished just a little bit earlier, Tony 10 would have blown away all these cares. He would have been home and hosed.

To look at the fourteen-part accumulator he assembled on 27 October 2010, and to see what happened to it, is to get the clearest analogy possible between the story of the gambler and the myth of Sisyphus, pushing that rock all the way up the hill, only for it to roll back down again.

He takes €1,750, with his usual surgical exactitude, out of the incoming bundles of An Post notes, to place it on this fourteen-part accumulator. The very notion of fourteen results all going the right way on the one day is so outlandish, there should probably be a rule forbidding bookmakers accepting such bets, even if the punter is only having €1.75 on it, let alone €1,750.

But Tony 10 is so badly in need of a really large amount of money, he goes for it anyway. The bet mainly involves football matches, with a couple of games of tennis thrown in. They are not the better class of football matches, being mostly midweek Cup or League Cup games in England, Scotland, Italy, Holland and Belgium – indeed, four of them are in the Belgian Cup, which is quite a big ask if you're trying to win roughly €300,000.

It is going quite well nonetheless, with Arsenal easily beating Newcastle 4–0 in the English League Cup, and Celtic and Rangers leading St Johnstone and Kilmarnock respectively in the Scottish equivalent. He is able to follow these scores coming in on Sky Sports. Otherwise he is following the night's proceedings on the bet365 website, the one with the black, grey and green colour scheme that he finds so attractive, when betting is suspended. He is sitting at the kitchen table in Sandhills; Fiona is in the sitting room with Hailey.

In Holland, PSV are winning 2–0 at Vitesse Arnhem. In the Coppa Italia, Brescia are beating Cittadella 1–0, while Lazio are having no trouble knocking out Portogruaro Summaga 3–0. In Israel, Tony 10 correctly picks Maccabi Tel Aviv to beat Bnei Sakhnin. Meanwhile his two tennis matches are working out the way he wanted – Marcos Daniel defeats Nicolás Massú in straight sets in a Challenger event on clay in São Paolo, while Philip Kohlschreiber wins two sets to one against Tobias Kamke in the BA-CA Trophy on the indoor hard court of Vienna.

So it is the Belgian Cup on which the life of Tony 10 seems to be depending, and on one game in particular, the match between Standaard Wetteren and Lokeren, which is being watched by 2,000 people at the ground and the Lord knows how many hundreds of thousands on betting websites all around the world. It is 1–1 at half-time, Tony 10 needs Lokeren to win.

The other Belgian games are going his way. Club Brugge beat Lommel 3–1, Westerlo beat Roeselare 2–0, Lierse S.K. beat Rupel Boom 4–0, and Germinal Beerschot beat Eendracht Aalst 4–0. It sounds easy when you write them all down like that, but for Tony 10 to be getting thirteen legs of this accumulator up is an almost superhuman feat of punting. And yet it will be of absolutely no use to him unless Lokeren can get the winner at Wetteren. Meanwhile in Scotland, just to fry his brain a little bit further, there is news on Sky Sports of St Johnstone scoring against Celtic, who were two goals up and are now leading 3–2.

On the sixty-ninth minute, Benjamin De Ceulaer makes it 2–1 for Lokeren. 'Watching' it on his laptop, Tony 10 is keeping an eye on all the other games, and they are still going well for him. Celtic are holding on to their lead. So this Lokeren result is looking like the one that will decide everything. The one that can send 300 grand into his account – 300,000 notes of the most merciful release — if only Lokeren can keep winning this match.

Four minutes later, Jan De Langhe equalises for Wetteren. There are still about twenty minutes left, including injury time. There may also be extra time, as this is a Cup game, but Tony doesn't care about that, he needs the win within the ninety minutes.

He doesn't get it.

Maddeningly, he has to sit there as the game drains away and no further scores are added in ordinary time. Mortifyingly, he sees the betting suspended a few times, his adrenaline pumping as he waits to see the outcome, to see if it's the goal for Lokeren that will fix everything for him, only to find that the betting resumes again at the same prices, that it's a false alarm, a near-miss of some kind. Excruciatingly, he is that one goal in a small-time football match in Belgium away from turning it all around. Some journeyman pro called Jan De Langhe, who will end up playing for most of the lesser football teams of Belgium, just cost him €300,000.

Lokeren win the tie in extra time, the final score 4–2. So Tony 10 does pick that winner too, he just picks it the wrong way. The drowning man has come so close to dry land, but once more he is struggling wildly, looking at a distant shore.

The next morning, just before 11.00 a.m., he lodges another €1,500 into his Paddy Power account, and he is off again.

CHAPTER 13

They come down again in the middle of December, the auditors. Two men in his office, two on the counters. They will surely find him out this time.

He knows they're going to get him. He is sitting at his desk in his office while the team sets about its business, and he knows for sure that at some point they are going to find this €294,000 that should be there, but that isn't there anymore.

They have come down from Portlaoise in the bad weather. He had a vague hope that a major fall of snow might save him today's ordeal. The weather is horrible, but it is not horrible enough to stop them getting to Gorey and setting about their task, while Tony 10 sits there, trying to look unconcerned.

He is sick with the fear. He is just waiting for them to get to the part where they discover that €294,000 is missing, and then he presumes he will end the day – end his life as he has known it – being led away in handcuffs.

He is waiting, just waiting …

There is one thing that he can do, something so pathetic it is really not worth doing at all, but he decides to do this thing anyway, maybe from some primal instinct of self-defence in the face of overwhelming odds. Or maybe just to pass the time doing something other than waiting.

He goes to the toilet. He needs to go to the toilet anyway, because of the sickness that is running through him, but he has this other reason, too, for absenting himself. While the auditors are checking the cash, on the quiet he takes two

Accountable Receipts (A.R.s) from a cupboard, thinking he might doctor them in some way before they get to them, a hope so forlorn that when he reaches the toilet and closes the cubicle door behind him, the first thing he does in this haze of fear and panic is to take out his phone and to send a text to Fiona: *I'm sorry.*

It feels like the end, that there's no way back from here. It feels like the end, here in this toilet cubicle in the post office in Gorey, not in one of the more salubrious venues in the gambler's imagination, not in the casino at Monte Carlo or a private box at Ascot – just here, locked in this cubicle, in the most appalling trouble, the adrenaline running madly as he is sending the text, knowing that it cannot be unsent. *I'm sorry.* The arrival of this onto Fiona's phone will surely, all by itself, start a process of disclosure that will lead to the end of this insanity. But he takes a black pen out of his inside pocket anyway, and he starts to change the figures. He changes a 5 to an 8, or he just puts a number in front of another to make it ten times bigger, trying in the most basic way imaginable to conceal his losses.

Part of him would like to throw away the pen and come out with his hands up, to give up this wretched pretence. Again he has this sense that, along with the ruination of his life, there is some kind of a black farce being played out here too, with this changing of the figures reminding him again of Lloyd Christmas in *Dumb and Dumber*. Except Lloyd would think it's a really clever idea, Tony 10 at least still has the awareness to know that this is futile, and that he is doomed. Yet he still proceeds with the task of falsification, driven not by any rational energy, just by some primitive rush of desperation. Gambling wildly that this might somehow postpone the inevitable day of judgement.

The despairing task completed, he tries to keep these new numbers in his head as he rejoins the activity in the office, sliding the A.R.s back into the cupboard and using the computer at his desk to bump up the figures in accordance with the changes he has made – to 'balance' these fictional books.

Somehow he makes the numbers on paper match the numbers on the computer, and somehow, astonishingly, he gets through this audit too. He thinks he may have got lucky in a couple of ways. Some very large investments had come into the post office that week, perhaps drawing attention away from other figures. And he wonders if the bad weather was in his favour too, he imagines the auditors being slightly distracted from their task by the prospect of driving back to Portlaoise on icy roads. In truth, he doesn't know how it happened, except that it did happen, and now he remembers that he sent that text to Fiona. *I'm sorry.*

He has told her he is sorry, but he has not told her what he is sorry about. He has the drive home to figure this one out. He is so broken down by it all, so utterly shattered, he wants to tell her the whole story. But he has been keeping this thing to himself for so long, he just can't let it go. Even in this most desperate situation, there is still some notion in his head that he can still get out of this – that if he can hide €294,000 from the auditors in the way that he did, it mightn't be completely beyond him to pick the few winners that would complete the job for him.

That he is driving home at all this evening feels to him like a miracle. Certainly when he was in that toilet cubicle, fixing the numbers, he could see no way that the day could finish like this. He is still wired, still traumatised, but slowly his rational mind is starting to function again. He starts to work out what he will say to Fiona when he gets home.

He says to Fiona that he is sorry about the way he's been lately, how withdrawn, how self-absorbed. She accepts what he is saying, because it sounds right, and indeed he is sorry about all that. But with all this other stuff he is still carrying around in his head, it may be some time before he can become more sociable.

◆ ◆ ◆

In the weeks around Christmas 2010 and the New Year, Ireland is still freezing. There are many who are confined to their homes by the bad weather, and in Carlow this is the case for most people. But not for Tony 10.

There's a particularly awful day, just before Christmas, when hardly anyone but the emergency services are out there. Nonetheless, Tony 10 has to get from Carlow to Gorey no matter what the Met Office says, no matter what warnings are going out from the Gardaí that all journeys, other than the most essential, are to be avoided. Tony 10 has no trouble including his journey in that category. He has the system in his office organised to such an extent, he can hide most of the evidence of wrongdoing, even from the auditors. But the thing is, he has to be there. If somebody else is obliged to open the office and to run it for a few days because he can't get there on account of the weather, all sorts of discrepancies could be found, and bad things could happen.

He has to be there, which means he has to get himself there in his black Volkswagen Polo, even though he has to start at 5.00 a.m., on a journey that usually takes an hour but today will take about four hours – if he gets there at all.

If he does get there, then on this day at least, he is saved. Even if the snow keeps falling for a week, he can stay in a hotel in Gorey, and he will be in control of this situation – if a man whose losses are moving towards the half-a-million mark can be said to be in control of anything.

These days he has to be wary not just of the weather but of the most mundane misfortune that might stop him getting into the office. Despite all the worry, which is clearly bad for his health, making him look bloated and generally unwell, he can't afford to get sick. Or at least, not sick enough that he can't drag himself somehow into work. When he is playing football he is mindful of the fact that an injury might immobilise him for a few days. His football is suffering anyway because he is always anxious about the result of some bet he has to check on his phone at half-time, part of him relieved if the bet has gone down so that at least he can concentrate on his own game in the second half.

But the snow … it feels like the very elements are his enemy now, that this snow will bring it all down on him, will be his ruination. It is pitch dark when he gets up out of bed to undertake this journey, one that any normal person would regard as impossible even in the clearest light of day. But Tony 10 can't wait for the light of day. He figures that by then, it will be too late. For the car to start on this freezing morning is remarkable in itself, then to get it out onto the road and pointed in the general direction of Gorey is difficult, but to keep it going on that road for the next few hours without being killed in some extremely horrible way is really quite a staggering achievement.

He can't rightly explain how he gets there, but he does it. For long stretches he is driving blind, he is losing control of the car and skidding and getting stuck in the snow, he is freezing and he is frightened, and yet the old Polo seems to be responding to his terrible need to keep going.

He makes it. He is able to stay in control of things in the office. There is no way he can make it back to Carlow tonight, though. He ends up staying in the Ashdown Park Hotel in Gorey for two nights. For him, this is not emergency accommodation, it is a form of sanctuary.

He finally makes it home to Carlow on Christmas Eve.

◆ ◆ ◆

After Christmas and into 2011, the betting shoots off into another realm, one in which reality no longer has any function. To get a proper sense of what is happening, perhaps it is best to start just after Christmas and to go through them one by one, all these bets that Tony 10 is having in the last week of 2010. And to recall that this activity is being facilitated by bookmakers who are aware that this is not the account of Tony O'Reilly the well-known tycoon, but Tony O'Reilly the manager of a post office in Co. Wexford.

He starts with a flourish on the Boxing Day football and racing, depositing €2,045 on a seven-part accumulator featuring Anderlecht, Celtic, Cardiff, Man United, Millwall, QPR and Wycombe Wanderers. It loses, but his next deposit, of €1,500 on a five-part 'acca' with Celtic, Cardiff, Hull, Rangers and Conegliano, wins €13,153.

He reinvests €1,150 on a losing double with Spurs and Gent, but wins €6,860 on a €2,000 treble with Spurs, Trentino and Virtus Bologna. He now has €16,863 in his account. He ends the day with a €1,863 loser on the New York Giants in the American football on Sky Sports, which still leaves him sleeping on €15,000.

The next morning he has €2,000 on *September Wind* to win a race at Turffontein in South Africa. It returns €4,800, bringing his balance up to €17,800. He loses €800 on

Tiereville at Deauville, and then goes for a €2,000 four-part acca on football and horses that eventually yields €4,172. It is not yet 11.00 a.m.

Another €2,000 double on the horses goes down, but a €3,000 double comes up, leaving him with €18,239.

At lunchtime a €2,000 straight bet on *Heresillie* to win at Southwell returns €8,000, and €1,239 on *Colorus*, also at Southwell, returns €4,956, bringing him up to €27,956 overall. Then he places €956 on *Knock On Wood* at Turffontein, €415 on *Dontpaytheferry* and €2,000 on the darts player Ronnie Baxter, which brings the balance up to €32,915. Later in the afternoon a €2,000 losing acca and a €3,000 winning double on rugby matches bumps this total up to €36,949.

On then into the evening, and a €2,949 double on Arsenal and the darter Colin Lloyd goes down, as does a €2,000 single bet on darter Mark Dudbridge, but a €4,000 straight win on Arsenal moves the balance up to €39,500. He loses €2,500 on Per Laursen in the darts, but that €4,172 from the morning's four-part accumulator on horses and football now kicks in, moving the total to €41,172.

In two days he wins about forty grand, but he has not finished the second day yet.

There's a €2,172 late-night loser on Georgia in the American basketball, and then a losing €4,000 double on Georgia and the cricketer Jonathan Trott to score a certain number of runs in an over – a swift six grand or so knocked off the balance by midnight, leaving €35,000 in the tank. It's nearly one in the morning and a €3,000 double on American racing and American football goes down, as does a €3,000 treble on American football and cricket and soccer. He is back to €29,000 at close of play.

At eleven the next morning he has a €5,000 double on *Faithful Ruler* to win at Lingfield and QPR to beat Coventry

City away. He will know the result by early afternoon. He has a €4,000 double on two horses, which will lose. He has a €5,000 five-part acca on the darts and the football, and it will lose. And yet despite dropping €9,000 so quickly, by 7.45 p.m. he is looking at a balance of €84,434.

This is because he has winners, too. At noon he has a €5,000 double on his old friends QPR and on *So Young* to win at Leopardstown, which returns €25,208. He has a €5,000 racing double on *Al-Fatowah* and *State Benefit*, which returns €16,100. He has €2,000 in a single bet on *Golden Sunbird*, who wins by a head at Limerick and returns €6,000. And that double on QPR and *Faithful Ruler* puts back another €16,100 into the coffers, bringing the total up to €84,434. Far more than a year's salary, racked up in a frenzy of betting on the post-Christmas sport.

A loss of €4,434 on a football double that evening takes the shine off it slightly, but he's still got an even €80,000 in there as midnight approaches. By two in the morning he has lost €10,000 of that in two bets, of €7,500 and €2,500, on American basketball games. And at some point in the dead zone between waking and sleeping, at 4.50 a.m. he 'invests' €10,000 in a six-part acca on the next day's football, darts, and racing. That bet will go down.

At 11.30 the next morning, 29 December, with €60,000 in his account, Tony 10 kicks off with a €5,000 double on *Big Game Hunter* to win at Limerick and on the Egyptian football team Haras El Hodoud. It goes down, but he is waiting on the result of another €5,000 double on Haras El Hodoud and on *Cottrelsbooley* to win at Leopardstown. Meanwhile he loses a €10,000 acca with seven parts, comprising football, darts, and racing. He is chasing now. He had more than €80,000 last night, it is down to €50,000 by noon, so he figures this €10,000 acca will make it right.

It doesn't. Moreover he drops another €5,000 on *Captain Chris* at Newbury.

Then he gets a couple of winners. A single bet of €5,000 on *Grasp Your Destiny* returns €17,500 – again, the name of the horse suggests that Tony 10 is starting to back them just because he likes the name. A punt of €7,500 on *Grandouet* at Newbury returns €15,750, so that he's got a fairly respectable €55,750 in there by 1.00 p.m.

Then €5,570 goes on *Darwins Fox* at Limerick, followed by another €10,000 lost on a four-way acca involving horses and darts. But then that double on *Cottrelsbooley* and Haras El Hodoud throws in €24,750, and a racing/darts treble, featuring *Big Zeb* winning the big one at Leopardstown, brings in €50,000. Thus in the middle of the afternoon, Tony 10 is looking at six figures in his balance: €100,650.

It is still a lot less than he needs, though, which is that €300,000, moving in the direction of half-a-million.

Within two hours, by 5.25 p.m., he takes that balance of €100,650 down to €35,000. He manages this with a €2,000 double, and single bets of €4,000 and €10,000 on the horses; €4,650 on a darts double featuring Gary Anderson and Andy Hamilton; two €10,000 trebles on football and darts; a €15,000 acca on seven football and rugby matches; and a €10,000 single bet on *Mi Regalo* at Kempton, the result of which will not be known till 5.37 p.m.

Mi Regalo wins a six-furlong sprint at a price of 7/2 and returns €45,000. The balance is back to €80,000.

It is quite an afternoon of sport, and Tony 10 is not going to stop now.

The evening's fare brings a winning €5,000 double on the rugby team Bayonne and the horse *Insolenceofoffice*, which yields €11,307, and a return of €14,000 for an outlay of €4,000 on some tennis proposition. There are losses, though:

€5,000 on Fernando Torres to score; €4,000 and €7,000 on two horses in the American racing; and €10,000 on a four-way acca on the darts and American basketball.

He is down around the €70,000 mark now, and a spate of lost €1,000s on the casino games knocks another €10,000 off this, sending him back to the late night racing from America. A bet of €5,000 goes down, as do four bets of €10,000 each, until a €5,000 bet on *Special Knight* returns €37,000 and €10,000 on *Celluloid Hero* rakes in €44,000, restoring the balance to €70,000.

So it's after one o'clock in the morning now, and he's back up to €70,000. He tries €10,000 on a basketball treble. At 3.40 a.m. that treble returns €55,000, sending him to bed for a few hours with the not unhappy thought that he's got €115,000 in his Paddy Power account.

When he gets to the laptop again in the morning, he finds that a €16,000 basketball double he had placed earlier on the Los Angeles Lakers and Oklahoma State has turned into €164,449, which includes €10,000 returned to him from the previous night's racing for a non-runner.

He is roughly halfway from where he needs to be, and of course he is more than halfway to somewhere else entirely.

It's now 30 December, lunchtime, and he's off again, with a fighting fund of €164,449. He uses it mostly on the racing – with the odd tennis or darts match thrown in.

He is losing in the early stages on the horses at Lingfield, Taunton, Limerick and Down Royal: €4,449 going down on *Edgeworth*, €10,000 on *Yes Tom*, €10,000 on *Perfect Reward*, €10,000 on *Luddsdenene*, €10,000 on a racing/tennis treble, €10,000 on a six-part acca that contains a bit of everything, and €20,000 on *Fools Wildcat* at Leopardstown. That's nearly €75,000 gone in less than two hours.

Necessity, the horse, puts €35,000 back in there, for a stake of €10,000. *Tell Halaf* kicks in another €48,750 in another bad race at Lingfield (the race itself was worth €1,706 to the winner) for an outlay of €15,000. This raises him up again to €148,750.

From this, €8,750 goes on *Judgthemoment* at Kempton, ridden by Eddie Ahern, who will be banned for ten years after the ride he gives the same horse at Lingfield a few weeks later. A further €10,000 and then €15,000 goes on football and racing trebles, and €15,000 goes on a five-part acca, one part of which involves Wydad Athletic, a football club in Morocco.

Tony 10 is now in the market for €15,000 five-part accumulators, which might include a football club in Morocco.

Another €7,600 goes down on a six-parter, which again includes Wydad Athletic, and as the evening arrives there are losses of €12,400 on a football treble, €10,000 on a football/darts combination and €20,000 on a seven-part acca, mostly football. By 10.00 p.m. Tony 10 is down to fifty grand.

So far, on this one day, he is losing more than €100,000. But it goes on. He loses €4,600 on a five-part darts and basketball acca, and €5,400 on another five-part acca on football matches in places such as Mexico and Israel.

He starts the next day, New Year's Eve, at 6.45 a.m. with a loss of €10,000 on a four-part acca, mostly tennis. At 9.45 a.m. another €10,000 goes on a seven-part acca of tennis and football. He now has a total of €20,000 in his account, a 'mere' €20,000.

Around noon, €10,000 of this goes on a five-part football acca, and then the last €10,000 goes on a horse called *Woop Woop*, on the all-weather track at Lingfield. He 'led inside final furlong, headed 50 yards out, kept on' to finish second. If *Woop Woop* had won, the first prize was just over €2,000, which means that the stake of this punter in Gorey is five times higher than the value of the race to the winner.

By early in the afternoon of 31 December, Tony 10, who the previous day had €164,448 to his credit, is back to zero.

At 2.19 p.m. he makes a fresh deposit of €5,000.

CHAPTER 14

To write those numbers down, and to read them, is to feel a sense of deep unease, as if you've found yourself in some place you've never been before, a place in which €10,000, €15,000, €164,449, are just vague concepts which have lost all meaning.

You worry that you might be losing some perspective yourself, as you rattle through an afternoon of five-figure sums being punted as if there was some underlying logic to it, which in a way there was – it's just that it was the logic of a different universe, a desperate place in which a man keeps looking frantically for the exit, for the way home, knowing deep down that there is none. That he can never get back there.

He has only a vague connection now with a time when €15,000 would be a lot of money to have in your possession in one lump, the sort of money that could improve your life in some significant way, maybe through buying a car or getting rid of a heap of debts. These days €15,000 is his stake on a seven-part accumulator – it's just a passing fancy in an orgy of gambling. He is too far gone to be even thinking about buying cars or about paying back debts of a mundane kind. Not with the debt that is hanging over him.

In the early weeks and months of 2011, he is waiting for that call, waiting to be caught. He has a headache all the time due to this constant pressure of the winning and the losing, and the incessant anxiety is making him physically sick. But he can't even begin to think of getting sick officially, of taking a day off from that office in which all of his black secrets are hidden. He is locked into this zone in which all the losing, over a long period of time, has drastically lowered his expectations, so that the wins feel better than they should feel – so that, in a twisted way, the losing is creating this desire, this craving for more action, for the exaggerated release of the win.

He finds no peace even when he walks Jack through the grounds of the College. He is breaking out in rashes, he is putting on weight due to stress and then losing weight because he can't eat. He is feeling like this every day. There is a certain black humour in the fact that he can count the days in a beautiful diary from the Paddy Power organisation, which is sent to him by registered post.

In this diary, which is probably the nicest one that he has ever seen, he can look forward to the important events of the sporting year. In truth, though, he is finding it hard to cast his mind beyond the next race, the next five races. And beyond that, he can look forward mainly to the next visit from a team of investigators, whenever it comes, as it surely must. At which point he figures his diary in general may need to be radically rearranged.

He still has this actual life to which he is vaguely connected, with a wife and a baby daughter, Hailey, with whom he experiences moments of peace and joy. These moments are all the more poignant for the fact that there is something he knows that Hailey doesn't know, something that he fears will change the way she sees him for the rest of her life. He sits there with her sometimes, holding her as she goes asleep, and she looks up into his eyes, and for a few seconds there is this perfect connection between them, and there is not a single thing wrong with the world. And then his heart is sick again, when he thinks of all the trouble that is surely coming, when he wonders what kind of a future she will have as the daughter of this character who threw away everything that was good in his life, because he just couldn't stop gambling.

There is an instrumental track called 'Living' by Moby, about seven minutes long, that he plays to help her get to sleep. It is their song. It's got a wistful air to it, this soft guitar sound that seems to work for Hailey, for both of them in their endlessly vulnerable states. He films Hailey going to sleep in his arms while this music is playing, so that in the future they will have these moments at least, preserved from a time before it all changed.

From his deteriorating relationship with Fiona, he does not know what will remain to be preserved. Like most addicts, he is becoming a very difficult person to live with. His moods are constantly switching, one day he is euphoric, the next day he is destroyed, sometimes it even switches from hour to hour.

His isolation, his need for secrecy, his desire just to be left alone most of the time with his obsession, are not just damaging the normal flow of their relationship, they are leading him to create arguments over nothing, just to get out of the house and down to the bookies. Although the irregular hours and general upheaval that comes with a new baby might explain some of the friction between them, Tony's addiction on top of all that is the silent force that is tearing them apart.

The arrival of the baby does provide him with an excuse when anyone remarks on his poor physical state – an excuse, too, to take himself into the spare room in the early hours of the morning, supposedly to give Fiona more space in the bed with Hailey, in truth to give himself more space to gamble. Other times, he lets Fiona sleep while he gives Hailey her night-feed, keeping an eye on his phone for the American racing and basketball.

The various pressures on them, both visible and invisible, are increasing this sense that Tony and Fiona are living in the same house but not living together. Most of the time Fiona sleeps with Hailey in the main bedroom while Tony 'sleeps' in this other room, with his beloved laptop, with Paddy Power.

And in that room he is packing away all his books and his CDs and his DVDs in that orderly way of his, either a sign that his obsessive neatness has entered some drastic new phase, or that he is physically preparing to make his exit, or some tormented combination of both. Certainly the neatness would not be unusual, and as for the exit, there is still nobody either close to him or at work who has any idea why he might be contemplating such a thing. It is all going on in the mind of one man, all the time.

When he has to be sociable, when he has no other option, he can still perform the role of a man with a fairly normal gambling habit, like on the Sunday when Fiona's parents are in the house and Arsenal are drawing with Liverpool, which would be the result that he wants. He is cheering on Liverpool, as a fan, but also because he needs them to keep Arsenal out so that he can collect on an accumulator. 'A few hundred,' he tells them, leaving the house with a few minutes to go in the match, to get down to the betting office so he can pick up a few thousand, not 'a few hundred', and immediately lodge it to his online account for the evening.

He is just entering the betting office when Arsenal score a goal, a penalty. He is distraught. It seems too late in the game for Liverpool to come back, but in fact there is a lot of injury time and as Tony 10 is trying to deal with the pain of the prospect of an evening without gambling, Liverpool get a penalty, a really lucky one, scored by Dirk Kuyt. He makes his lodgement of several thousand, then he returns to the house, giving off the positive vibes of a man whose team got a late equaliser and who made 'a few hundred' into the bargain.

Thus he is still managing to keep it all from Fiona, but outside of the house and the workplace he can get a bit careless. Niall Byrne is starting to notice that when they are playing poker with a few friends in Scraggs, Tony is so distracted by whatever is happening on his phone, he is hardly paying attention at all to the card-game, absentmindedly declaring 'all-in' for nearly every hand. Niall tackles him about it a few times, calling him 'All-In Tony.'

Like Niall, Tony's sister Sandra is also starting to notice that her brother seems deeply attached to his phone these days. She figures he may be struggling with some sort of a problem, the nature of which eludes her for now – but there is definitely something that disturbs her about Tony and his pathological use of the smartphone. His obsession with it seems to go beyond the 'normal' level of obsession common to so many people these days.

Sandra recalls that in any picture taken at that time in which Tony appears, either knowingly or unknowingly, you can see this vacant expression, you can tell that he isn't really 'there'. But still she is far away from guessing the true nature of the problem, and the vastness of it. Indeed, she still has the impression that as regards gambling, he is pretty good at it. He has managed to let enough people know about his victories, whereas nobody except the bookies know of his sickening defeats.

And even the part about him being good at gambling is correct, up to a point. He still has that talent for 'pricing' an event. He can figure out what the odds should be with such accuracy, in a better arrangement he would have been on the other side of the deal, himself a bookie. But either way, the fact that he is now deeply addicted makes it irrelevant how good he is, at anything.

Niall Byrne gets another inkling of this when they are driving to a football match in Hacketstown. It is about 10.00 a.m. on a Sunday morning and Tony is in the passenger seat, on his phone, as always, talking about some football match that day in Germany, something about Bayern Munich. While they both have a huge interest in football, Niall never knew Tony to care much for the German variety. So Niall is starting to suspect that 'All-In Tony' may be developing a few gambling issues, but again he has not an iota of the scale of it, and where it might he heading.

Tony 10 alone knows that. He has this life as Tony O'Reilly, but really he has become entirely Tony 10, living in his own head, which is scrambled to such an extent that many times when he is driving into work he is watching episodes of *Prison Break* on a portable DVD player, just to keep his head busy with something other than thoughts of gambling. Not pulling in to the side of the road, but watching it while he drives, the DVD player up against the windscreen. On the drive home in the evenings, by which time he has usually lodged funds in his account, always on the passenger seat beside him is the laptop, to keep an eye on the in-play betting. In more conscientious moments he would pull in to the hard shoulder to place a bet, and then resume his journey.

When he gets to work he must maintain this persona of the man in charge. To do this he must use all the instincts that got him there – getting things done efficiently, talking fast in that steetwise way of his. Keeping up the appearance of being the man in charge is essential now because the actual taking of the money is becoming reckless, it has to be given the quantities in which he is dealing. There's no more of the delicate operations to extract notes from a bundle with a pair of pliers. He is now depositing ridiculously large bundles of notes in his account in the Paddy Power office, and then fixing the figures in the post office to make it all balance as best he can.

He is compelled to keep gambling because he has created this circular hell for himself, whereby his only hope of a way out is to keep doing it, until, for whatever reason, he can't do it anymore. And indeed, there are a few days in March, and again in April, when he believes that he is not too far from finding that way out.

In two demented days, 5 and 6 March, his balance touches €172,000. A €15,000 acca returns €67,000; a €10,000 treble returns €41,311; a bet of €12,500 on a horse called *Uncle Junior* at Gowran Park returns €40,265; an €8,000 acca on eight football matches returns €88,823; a €15,000 acca on five different sports returns €95,454; a €10,000 treble, which includes an ice hockey game, returns €66,000; and a €12,000 treble returns €53,329, remarkable also for the fact that it features a team called Rain Or Shine Elasto Painters, a basketball club in The Philippines.

And yet, astoundingly, despite all these huge wins, by 6.00 p.m. on 6 March he is making a deposit again, this time of €4,000.

When you're betting €10,000 or €15,000 at a time, and you're betting more or less constantly, this can happen – especially when a balance of €172,000 has become relatively useless to you, given where you need to be, which by early April is roughly at the €900,000 mark.

It is hard to get there, almost a million euro, especially for a desperate man. But on a certain night in April, he feels that he might just be able to do it.

◆ ◆ ◆

It happens to most punters at some stage, they have an extraordinarily good run. For a little while, they just seem to have the magic. For a weekend in April 2011, when he is most in need of it, Tony 10 has the magic.

Staring with a deposit of €4,000 at lunchtime on the Friday, over the course of this weekend he lands several enormous winners, mostly accumulators that return very large five-figure and even the odd six-figure sums. And this time he is not letting it all slide at the usual rate, he is not incinerating all those gains in a blaze of ten-grand losers. This time he gets to €100,000, to €200,000, and he keeps going upwards.

He is calling them so well, he has €20,000 'in-running' on Charl Schwartzel to win the Masters, at 3/1. So he goes for Schwartzel just as he is winding up for a late surge that will see him birdie the last four holes at Augusta and win his first major – a swift profit of €60,000 there for Tony 10. After a couple of days of continual success, his balance stands at just over €280,000.

And it keeps getting better, until he is just under €400,000, waiting for the fourth leg of a tennis and football accumulator to take him up towards €450,000. Waiting on Zaragoza.

This is the one he remembers most fondly, sitting in the kitchen in Sandhills with Jack, watching Real Zaragoza playing Getafe. It's not even the amount that he stands to win, because he's winning fifty grand and more quite a lot these days, it's the fact that it will continue this great run, and it will get him halfway to where he needs to be. And if he gets there, he can start to believe that this might be doable, that salvation is possible.

The other parts of the acca are already in, they involved three tennis matches the details of which should not concern any sane person. Now he is watching Real Zaragoza taking the lead and then going two goals up within twenty-five minutes. But of course it is never going to be that easy, with Getafe getting one back just before half-time. And so Tony 10 only has to endure another forty-five minutes in order to receive this great psychological lift, to get halfway to what now seems like paradise, but what in the real world is simply zero – nothing gained but nothing lost either.

When the game ends 2–1 for Zaragoza, he is elated enough to lift Jack onto his shoulders and to do a little dance around the kitchen with him. Now he is looking at the number €448,408 in the top left-hand corner of his Tony 10 account, and by the early hours he has increased this to €462,000, making a profit on the Argentinian tennis player Brian Dabul.

In the course of a long weekend, he turns €5,000 into €462,000. He has forty-six winning bets out of 116 placed. He is starting to feel invincible again.

The next morning, in the office, he has visitors.

It is two men from the audit team in Dublin, but they are not there to do a full audit, they are engaged in setting up and testing a new An Post system for the delivery of cash. Still, for Tony 10 their presence in the same building is most unsettling. Indeed, when they arrive, it takes him a few minutes to realise that he has left his laptop open on his desk, with the Paddy Power website displayed on it. Naturally he had been hoping to forge ahead with this winning streak that he's on, but he is thwarted in this because the website seems to be down.

And then, as if the start of his day needed any more excitement, he receives a phone call from Paddy Power. Not just from someone representing the Paddy Power organisation, but from the man who tells him he is indeed Paddy Power, who mainly speaks for that corporation in its dealings with the media, a well-known national figure in his own right. He is calling Tony 10 on his mobile, telling him that if he wants to have a bet this morning, he can phone it in, and he can do this until such time as the website is running again. Furthermore he can use Paddy Power's personal mobile number for any such bets.

Tony is unable to engage properly with the conversation because as he is speaking to this man, he is looking at the members of the audit team and wondering if they are going to stumble upon the realisation that there is approximately €900,000 missing from this establishment – if you exclude the €462,000 that is, in theory, available on that Paddy Power website that is out of commission at present. So he can't be too talkative, in fact he doesn't want to be talking at all. He ends the call as calmly as he can in the circumstances.

The problem with the website is soon resolved, and by the afternoon he is betting online again.

◆ ◆ ◆

Perhaps the visit from the auditors, the phone call from Paddy Power, the sheer strangeness of it all has some unsettling effect, perhaps it increases his urge to keep accumulating as he had been doing, whatever it is, when Tony 10 starts up again, he is having no winners.

Before this day is done, he will lose €462,000.

Even during the boom you could buy a decent enough house in Carlow for €462,000, but Tony 10 punts it all away within twelve hours. The last €20,000 goes down just before 10.00 p.m. that night on some Brazilian tennis player called Thales Turini. Out of thirty-one bets placed, twenty-nine of them lose.

It is carnage.

It goes on all day, this bonfire of all that exists in the account of Tony 10, this systematic torching of €462,000. Bets of €20,000, €30,000 are standard. Names are appearing that seem to belong not to anything in the world that we know, but to some twisted satire – there's Negeri Sembilan, a football team in Malaysia, and Balestier Khalsa in Singapore, and Breidablik Kópavogur in Iceland, and Trenkwalder Admira in Austria. There's the under-20 team representing Kasımpaşa in Turkey, and there's the Belarus under-19s. There are tennis players such as Charalampos Kapogiannis and Daniel Muñoz de la Nava. There's a horse called *Shouldhaveknownbetter*, as in the Jim Diamond song, which was his mother's favourite, on which Tony 10 has €20,000, and which fulfils all the potential of his name by being tailed off at Taunton.

It is important to remember, though, that none of these results should be viewed in isolation. Just as there's a momentum when a punter starts winning, there are equal and opposite forces that take hold when things start going wrong. Panic, for a start, after the first €100,000 disappears, then this terrible fear when the losing doesn't stop at €200,000, and the chasing goes on and on, all the way down to that last €20,000, then oblivion. It happened to Tony 10 on that day when he lost it all at the Galway Races, a day which seems like such a long time ago now, when a mere €11,500 would have made everything all right.

Yes, it is carnage. But the punter can be at his most vulnerable when he is flush, thinking that he can do no wrong.

CHAPTER 15

After that long, long weekend when deliverance seemed so close, the highest number he reaches after this is €250,000. But even as he looks at a quarter of a million sitting in his account, he feels that, in all probability, he has already lost. That he is on the ropes, being pounded to a pulp, wondering when he's going to hear the bell. Maybe even hoping for the bell.

They have built a new branch of BoyleSports just down the road from where he lives. The place materialises so quickly, it seemed to have been built overnight. And one Friday night Tony drops in to this fine premises on his way to SuperValu to buy a bottle of milk and a packet of biscuits. While he is in this new BoyleSports, just out of habit he puts a €200 accumulator 'in-running' on a bunch of Irish football matches.

A few minutes later he is home again, having his tea and biscuits, checking the results coming in on his phone. He notes that he has won something in the region of €6,500 – a bad night for the management of the new office, but for Tony 10 it's just a reminder that he's in so deep now, he can take the local bookie for six-and-a-half grand in the time it takes him to organise a cup of tea and biscuits, and it hardly even registers with him. To the staff who would have to pay out the money, he must seem like some kind of a genius, hitting them with such a haymaker on a bunch of small-time football matches. What other attacks was he planning? What magic does he possess?

If they could have seen him as the results were coming in, virtually indifferent to his success, they would have realised that there wasn't much magic left in it these days. The fight is gone out of him now, he is utterly wasted. He is still trying to control everything in the office, but the stress of that is making him slightly careless in other ways. For example, there's the time Niall rings him on his mobile and he says he's at work, but when Niall ends the call he realises that Tony has not hung up properly – and Niall can hear the sounds of a betting office in the background. 'Why the fuck is he lying to me?'

Now Tony is giving in to the darkest imaginings. He keeps thinking of Hailey growing up while he is probably in jail, missing all that. And what will she think of him when she is able to form an opinion on what he has done? The father she was supposed to have was Tony O'Reilly, the man with an excellent job and every chance of continuing in an upwards direction, who could give her whatever she needed. The father she will have is this Tony 10, who has screwed up everything for himself and for her and for everyone belonging to him. How could he ever make it up to her?

He and Fiona are now strangers living under the same roof. He has separated himself from any normal vision of family life. He is becoming that zombie in the spare room. He is trying to function in the office while constantly watching the CCTV pictures from outside, which will tell him when the auditors are here again. Thursday is the day when they tend to arrive, so he starts to take Thursdays off, which in itself does not look good.

And then something else arrives, an invitation to the Aviva Stadium for the final of the Europa League on 18 May, between Porto and Braga. The Paddy Power corporation now regards Tony 10 as such a valued client, it dispatches this superb invitation pack, again by registered post, like the lovely diary, requesting the pleasure of his company in its executive box for this prestigious event. There is even a phone call from the relevant operative in Paddy Power, telling Tony 10 that two seats are available, if he can make it.

He decides he can make it, because at this stage he can't think of much reason not to make it. He's fucked anyway, he reckons, so he might as well get one night of VIP corporate hospitality out of it. So he arranges to go with a fellow manager in the Gorey branch, with whom he plays snooker at lunchtime. In anticipation, he has €500 on Radamel Falcao of Porto to score the first goal, at odds of 9/2.

They have the tickets, they have the itinerary. They arrive at the Aviva wearing jeans, casual and not overly smart. Tony sees this thing not as some networking opportunity, but more the kind of thing an addict does just before he checks in for treatment, a 'session' on the way to the rehab clinic, getting blotto one last time.

Bittersweet though it is, he enjoys the dreamlike nature of the evening. He finds pleasure in the surrealism of it, in savouring each moment, thinking nothing, for a few hours at least, of what surely awaits him. There are a dozen seats in the executive box, the other ten people do not necessarily look like high rollers, but they look well-to-do. They might be friends or relations of Paddy Power executives. But Tony and his companion from Gorey are largely keeping themselves to themselves, somewhat in awe of their exalted surroundings in this restricted zone to which they gain access via a lift, which transports them into this carpeted area with a supply of fine champagne and a steak dinner with silver service.

Falcao does score the first goal, meaning a profit on the night of €2,250, which at this stage means virtually nothing.

The following week there is another blowout for Tony 10 when he has €1,000 on Rooney and Messi to score in the Champions League Final between Manchester United and Barcelona at Wembley. He is watching the match in the front bar in Scraggs. He celebrates when Rooney scores in the first half, and he celebrates again when Messi scores in the second half, drawing the attention of other customers, who are amused at the sight of someone apparently supporting both teams. His bet of a thousand was at odds of 8/1. In this place that has meant so much to him over the years, he does that thing again of declaring that he has won considerably less than he has actually won, claiming a profit of €500 and buying a round of drinks for everyone in the bar. It's just like old times, though it might be the last time.

Tony 10 seems to be firmly established now as a favoured client with the Paddy Power corporation, because the next month he receives another beautifully presented invitation by registered post, this time to the Paddy Power box at the Curragh on 27 June for the Dubai Duty Free Irish Derby meeting. There are two VIP tickets enclosed, and indeed his local branch of Paddy Power in Carlow supplies him with another three 'ordinary' tickets for the day. But this time Tony is so sure he's about to get caught by the auditors, he gives the VIP tickets to Niall, planning to distribute the rest of the tickets among other friends. It should be noted that as the manager of a large and busy pub, Niall would receive such invitations in the normal course of things, and that Tony, too, as a prominent figure in the community might get these tickets without anyone close to him suspecting that he had earned them through being a high roller, let alone one who was thinking he was about to go down.

On the Sunday morning of the Derby he still hasn't been apprehended, and he is in the shower when his friends call to the house to collect the other tickets. Maybe because it is a spectacularly sunny day, maybe because he's still looking for that last blowout, he decides that he will go to the Curragh after all.

The Paddy Power executive box at the Curragh has a perfect view of the winning post, and the people gathered there to enjoy the view are the real high rollers. The lads from Carlow, in their jeans and open-necked shirts, are feeling somewhat out of their depth. Tony looks across the room and sees Paddy Power himself standing there, then looks away quickly to avoid a potentially embarrassing conversation. These are all obviously rich people, or at least they give that impression, and some of them are serious gamblers. Indeed, the box of JP McManus is just next door, and Niall Byrne contrives to have his picture taken with McManus, the gambler's gambler.

Yet the one who for some time has been one of the biggest gamblers of them all, Tony 10, has almost no money. He will later learn that so many millions were going in and out of his account, he was regarded by the Paddy Power corporation as being one of an elite grouping of gamblers which included a couple of world-renowned sportsmen, the sort of fellows who would not be bracketed in any other setting with a post office manager from Gorey.

Today at the Curragh, the post office manager is not punting tens of thousands anymore, he has lost €600 online on the races, though he does have €100 back home, in cash, for a few drinks that evening. There is a concierge who is looking after the needs of all the clients, and when he hears the little party from Carlow talking about heading off to get money out of the ATM, he arranges straightaway for €500 to be placed in 'Mr O'Reilly's' online account.

Mr O'Reilly loses that €500 immediately on the favourite in the next race.

But he sees this as his last hurrah, so what does it matter? There is no great change that a winning bet of €500 can make to his life at this stage. And if there is any doubt that he is letting go of everything, he ends up that night back in Carlow in a pub called Dicey Reilly's, doing karaoke. It's the final outbreak of pure escapism, this scene from a surreal ould fellas' session.

He knows what is coming. He thinks that if they didn't come for him last week, they must be coming next week.

He is right about that, too.

◆ ◆ ◆

It is 8.45 a.m. on Wednesday, 29 June 2011 when he gets the call. He is in Gorey, parking the Polo at the back gate of the post office, the one he sometimes used when he needed to nip out of work and into Paddy Power. The call is from a work colleague. He says he is looking for Tony because an audit team has already arrived at the post office. They are members of the Retail Control Team Regional Office East, to give them the full title.

The call is not by way of warning or any such thing, it is simply to inform Tony of this unusual situation, because this is the sort of thing a branch manager needs to know. How badly he needs to know it is something only Tony 10 understands.

He has been expecting this day of reckoning for so long, and yet when he hears those words on the phone he is sent into a state of panic, of utter confusion, which lasts for a few moments. It lasts just long enough for him to decide that the one thing he cannot do is to walk into that premises and give himself up to the Retail Control Team – still that image haunts him, of being led away in handcuffs from the office. Whatever is about to happen, he wants to avoid that particular horror-show.

When he gets through that moment of panic and makes that decision, he feels this enormous surge of adrenaline.

This is it.

He has this massive hit of heightened awareness and in a split-second he knows what he is going to do. He does not reply to the voice on the phone, as if he can't hear what his colleague is saying, allowing the call to break down. Then he texts back with the first wild thought that comes into his head. He texts that he has been in a road accident near Tullow, that the car is in a ditch and he is waiting for the Gardaí and an ambulance to arrive. He is so wired, he makes a few spelling mistakes in the text, which is uncharacteristic, but adds credibility to the notion that he is traumatised by the accident.

The instincts for avoiding detection that he has honed over the last few years are still working. He takes the sim card out of his phone and throws it on the floor in front of the passenger seat. He reckons that he might have two hours until the Team is able to establish the extent of the shortfall. Two hours at the most.

He had never imagined it like this. In his mind's eye, he had never seen himself in the car so near to the office when the hammer came down – he was either in the office or very far away from it, which is where he wants to be now.

Two hours.

This is it.

The adrenaline still rushes through him as he estimates that he could be out of the country in two hours, he could make it across the border in that time, he could get to the North. That is what he will try to do. He will try to make it to Belfast.

But right now he is still in Gorey, about twenty yards away from the building in which his fate is being determined. He could just walk in there and save them the trouble but he is beyond that now. He takes a few seconds to compose himself. And then he starts driving.

He drives out of Gorey, taking the back roads towards Arklow. He has the 9.00 a.m. news on the radio, still so pumped up he is half expecting to hear something about himself already, some warning to the public that this crazy man is on the run and they should stay clear of him.

A few miles outside Gorey he is driving so fast he meets a hump-backed bridge and the car bounces to the other side of the road. He is driving as dangerously now as he was on that morning when he made it through the snow from Carlow to Gorey, except this is now the height of summer, and there is no way back from here. The car very nearly flips onto its side, but he manages to keep it on the road. But the shock of so nearly losing control of the car, on top of all the other shocks, has a kind of a calming effect.

He stops at a petrol station. He attempts a rational assessment of what he has, and what he will need. He has about €700 in cash in the boot of the car, money he had taken from the post office the previous night to use for betting, except somehow he never got around to it. He even has some clothes in the boot, some ironing he had picked up from his mother. And he has his passport, which he has been carrying for some time, not with any specific plan in mind, more a reflection of the subconscious fear that he may have to get the hell out of the country at some point – but not like this, he had never seen it like this.

He fills the tank with petrol. Still consciously trying to slow everything down, he buys food, some Hunky Dorys buffalo flavour crisps and a few bars of Twirl chocolate. But he will not stop to eat them. He knows that they'll be looking for him soon.

◆ ◆ ◆

Tony O'Reilly Senior receives a call from the branch manager in Carlow Post Office, telling him that his son hasn't turned in for work in Gorey today. It is about 10 o'clock, Tony Senior feels there can be no good reason for this. His first thought is that there has been a tiger kidnapping. Fiona has been calling Tony and getting no reply, which is unusual. At about 11.00 a.m. she calls the office in Gorey and gets to speak to the colleague who forwards her the text that Tony had sent him about the 'accident'. Now she is seriously worried. She calls Niall, who in turn calls a friend of his who works in the ambulance service, asking him if he's aware of an accident anywhere on that road, maybe near Tullow, or Tinahely, or Shillelagh? There is no accident that the ambulance worker knows of, no black Volkswagen Polo in a ditch.

Around noon, Niall rings another friend of his whose father is a retired police officer. He makes a few calls and soon the word comes back to Niall that there has been a surprise audit in Gorey post office. Niall figures straightaway that this is no tiger kidnapping, that it must be about Tony and his gambling. All these scenes come back to him – the unnatural attachment to the phone, the constant shortage of money, the weird level of interest in what Bayern Munich might be doing, the day that Tony didn't hang up properly and he wasn't at work as he said, he was in a betting office. Niall describes all these signals now ringing together in his head … bing … bing … bing … bing … bing.

Niall and Tony Senior go out to Sandhills, to Fiona, who is distraught, but still absolutely convinced that this is a case of a tiger kidnapping. The Gardaí have declared a news blackout and are officially describing Tony O'Reilly as a Missing Person.

◆ ◆ ◆

Tony 10 does not know exactly how he will get to Belfast, except that he will keep driving northwards, driving away from everything. And as he tears up through County Wicklow and onto the M50 and past the city of Dublin and on through County Louth, he has this weird sense that he is in some kind of a *Thelma & Louise* situation, that his life has now officially become a movie, and that the car chase bit is underway.

It is not a movie, but he really does need to escape, and then he needs to figure out what to do next, choosing from a rapidly diminishing list of options. Astonishingly, he still needs to gamble.

The previous day he had €5,000 on an eight-part accumulator, mainly tennis, the result of which he will know by mid-afternoon. If it comes off, he will have roughly €45,000 in his Paddy Power account, nearly a year's wages for some men, perhaps enough to see Tony 10 through this weekend anyway.

He also has a winning docket from Paddy Power in Gorey that is worth €10,000, and while in theory he can cash this in in any branch of Paddy Power, he would prefer to wait until he has exhausted all other options. At this stage, even Paddy Power might identify him as a man with a bit of a problem and report his appearance in one of their outlets.

He gets to Dundalk by 11.00 a.m. He parks at a shopping centre, needing more supplies. He buys a new SIM card in a Vodafone shop for the dongle that will enable him to keep on betting online, and he picks up a Nike Mercurial baseball cap in a sports shop – a basic form of disguise, to be helped along by the fact that on this trip, he won't be shaving. Then he goes to a bank to change his €700 to sterling. His paranoia is so heightened, he is fearful of any security cameras. When the bank official behind the counter takes his money into a back office to get the sterling, he is sure that the transaction shouldn't be taking so long, sure that some description of him has already been issued, that his new baseball cap is not working.

Eventually, though, he leaves the bank with about £600, still apparently a free man, though by now the audit team has undoubtedly found what they were looking for. But there is nothing on the radio as he drives across the border and takes the motorway straight into Belfast.

He arrives in Belfast around lunchtime. He has been in this city once before, with a couple of friends, but he has no idea where he is going. All he knows is that he needs to get to the first betting office he can find, which happens to be a branch of Paddy Power located down some back street. He figures that a few bets might help to calm him down.

Using his sterling, he settles himself in the betting office and starts punting a hundred quid a time on the horses. He is also heading out from time to time to an internet café to check on the progress of various events in that eight-part accumulator on which so much is now depending. Even though it features exotica such as the USA ladies football team, somehow it is still standing, and by 3.00 p.m. all the results will be in, and the truth will be known.

His cash betting, on the other hand, which is of more immediate importance, is not going well. Wherever he is staying tonight, he will have to pay in cash, to avoid using his credit card and thus giving a major clue to the authorities in two jurisdictions, which he assumes are now both looking for him. If the car journey had reminded him of something out of *Thelma & Louise*, he feels he is in some other movie now, in which he is putting his last 100 quid on a horse in the last race, desperately needing it to win. And in this movie, it does win – he has 600 quid again, which means he will be able to spend the night in a hotel and not in his car.

More than this, he will also be able to gamble online in a major way, because his accumulator has come up. He has €45,000 in his Paddy Power account.

Even now ... yes, even now ... as he moves around Belfast in disguise, having fled the country that morning, his life in smithereens ... even now he is thinking that with €45,000 in there maybe, if he keeps gambling, he can get it all back. Or at least he can win a large amount of it, and thus pay back a significant chunk of the money he has stolen. Always, always, he just wants to get back to where he started, or at least to within, say, a hundred miles of it.

He really thinks he can still do it. But first he needs to find a place to hide.

Fiona and Niall go driving that afternoon and through the evening to Tullow and beyond, to any shop along the way that might have some CCTV footage, anything at all. Niall figures that over the next twenty-four hours they cover most of the county of Wexford. In particular, those parts of it near the coast.

It is one of those hellish experiences that no human being ever wants to go through, and now they are going through it. Will they find the missing person or a dead body? What the fuck has he done, and what the fuck is he doing now? Is there still some point to this desperate searching, or is it already too late?

◆ ◆ ◆

Tony 10 drives the Polo into a multi-story car park near to a Premier Inn, the sort of hotel that is attractive to him because it seems impersonal. Like they don't care where you're coming from, or where you're going to. Except it doesn't work out like that. When he arrives at the reception desk, thinking that he won't be calling himself Tony O'Reilly, that he is now Niall Byrne, the receptionist tells him they would need to see some form of identification.

Tony figures he cannot furnish them with his passport or any other such documents, because he assumes he is now on a proverbial Wanted poster. Or maybe an actual one. Not wanting to assist his pursuers in any way, he tells the receptionist that unfortunately he hasn't got any documents of that nature on him right now, and it is too inconvenient to go away and get them. He is trying to discern anything in the manner of the receptionist that might suggest she knows well who he is without any ID, but even in his state of paranoia he senses this is nothing more than the routine procedure in such a 'corporate' establishment.

He goes back to the car park, thinking he will need to find somewhere a bit less corporate. With the evening descending he drives out onto the streets of Belfast again, and he sees a sign for Carrickfergus, eleven miles away.

He decides to head for Carrickfergus.

Maybe he is drawn by the sea, or by the song, that saddest of all songs, but here too as he drives into the town he finds something that he wasn't expecting – it is the marching season, and the place is festooned with Union Jacks. As if he hasn't enough complications in his life already, Tony is aware that he is driving what is probably the only car in Carrickfergus at this time with a Southern registration. With no alternative but to accept the black humour of the situation, he parks outside Dobbins Inn Hotel, a cosy-looking old establishment on the High Street, near the sea, and books in under the name Niall Byrne.

The woman at the desk does not ask him for identification. He says he is just travelling around for a few days. She says it will be £50 a night. Tony's relief that the transaction has been so simple, that you can just check into a hotel without having to endure some heart-stopping event, lasts until he goes back to the car to collect his stuff, and finds that he has locked the keys in the car. Everything he needs, his money, his clothes, most of all his laptop, is in there. And the usual thing to do in such a predicament is to ask for the help of, say, the police.

He feels he is on the brink of irretrievable madness, if not over the brink. And then he realises that the boot of the car is still open. As nonchalantly as any fugitive gaining access to his car through the boot, gathering his belongings for what will probably be his last days of freedom, Tony O'Reilly or Tony 10 or Niall Byrne, or whoever he is at this stage, makes it through this part of the ordeal.

It is probably for the best that he is unaware of some of the history of Dobbins Inn. He doesn't know that over the years the ghost of a woman has allegedly been seen moving through Reception and into the old stone fireplace, or that guests have reported being woken up by the sensation of a hand touching their faces. There is enough of the abnormal going on in his life without getting into the paranormal.

He is in his hotel room, having a long bath, trying to comprehend the enormity of the fact that he is now a man on the run, about to become notorious, about to cause all sorts of trouble for everyone else in his life. But he is also hanging on to the thought that he has that €45,000 still in the online tank.

He stays in the bath for an hour, trying to calm down, trying to figure out how the hell he got here, knowing deep down that there is ultimately just one answer to that. It was Tony 10 who got him here, and in this weird zone which he now inhabits, his only coping mechanism is to become that character again, for as long as these desperate circumstances will permit. He figures that if it was Tony 10 who got him here, only Tony 10 can get him through it and out the other side. That no normal man, certainly not the man who was once Tony O'Reilly, could find a way of dealing with this world of shit.

After the chaos of the day, he is still in some state of shock. He knows that the storm is coming, but it hasn't broken yet. That these few hours, or few days, or whatever, before he is discovered may be the only time in which he knows some form of peace for the foreseeable future. Maybe he will never know such a thing again.

In the strangest way, it is starting to feel almost as if Tony 10 is on holiday. He lies on the bed watching a film on his iPod Classic, a documentary about England at Italia '90. He goes down to the hotel bar to have a couple of pints of Heineken. The news is on the television, but there is nothing about him.

Still he waits for the knock on the door. Still he is gambling. He bets through the evening at €5,000 a time, by 9.30 p.m. he bumps that €45,000 up to €60,000. By 11.00 p.m. this has come down to €28,000.

He manages to stop it there. He just can't face the thought of starting the following day at zero, deprived of the usual method of replenishing his funds. He keeps that money in his account overnight, ready to start again in the morning, if morning comes.

CHAPTER 16

Just before 8.00 a.m. he moves his car from the front of the hotel to the car park nearer the waterfront. He has this sense that he needs to keep moving the car, that to leave it outside Dobbins night and day with its Carlow registration would attract attention. Later he plans to move it back to the hotel, where the parking is free overnight. And then back again to the car park.

It's as if he's trying to bring some internal logic to this surreal situation. In a newsagent's he checks the papers, there is nothing about him, not yet. Like some massively stressed tourist, he thinks he should make the most of his time up here in this dreamworld, while it lasts. The weather is beautiful. He mightn't be able to enjoy a fine day for quite a while, so he strolls up to have a look at the famous Carrickfergus Castle, to take pictures. He buys the new Foo Fighters album, which he will play on his iPod.

He knows there will be consternation back home on the part of Fiona, on the part of his family and friends. He sees the emails from them coming in, but he just can't engage with them because … because he can't. He is too consumed with his own trauma, frozen in this weird space, unable to bring himself to communicate due to the enormity of his guilt and shame, and also because he is sure that any such contact will reveal his whereabouts, and will lead half the world to Carrickfergus. He is starting to have this notion that he might try to get across the water to Liverpool, but is worried he will be caught by the ferry customs people.

He does not seriously entertain thoughts of suicide, it is just a fleeting presence in his head, because he is an addicted gambler after all, and he still has that €28,000 in his online account.

But that is soon gone as well, as happens so quickly when you're banging out the accas at ten grand a time. By lunchtime he is looking at zero in the top left-hand corner, at that fathomless void into which he has thrown millions, thrown his very soul – but still he has hope. He is waiting on a four-part tennis accumulator, the result of which will not be known until teatime. Two parts of the acca are on doubles matches at Wimbledon, which means these are at least high-class events in which everyone is probably trying. But for the moment there is still zero in the account, zero euro and zero cent, a terrifying sight.

Tony 10 takes himself off to a Ladbrokes office to bet in cash for the afternoon, to wait on the result of that acca that will get him back up to €28,000 if it wins.

It turns out he is not doing badly at all, betting for the afternoon in Ladbrokes. He is a couple of grand up on the horses, but at this stage this is really just walking-around money. He is still waiting on the big one, waiting like he has done so many times before, with just that little bit more tension in his gut this time. Because if this one goes down, he is left with nothing but that Paddy Power docket for €10,000, and that will require a personal appearance in some branch office where they will have to check this large bet with the Gorey office, where he made it. And he doesn't want that.

At 5.48 p.m. he is back in his hotel room, mad with joy. The result is in, he is up again. He has precisely €28,800 in his account.

By 6.12 p.m. he is back to zero again.

His last ten grand in the online world is riding on these

six representatives – Mihaela Buzărnescu, the Romanian tennis player, the football teams Spartak Trnava of Slovakia, Ferencvárosi of Hungary and Viking FK of Norway, and the tennis doubles teams of Lindstedt/Tecău and Lisicki/Stosur.

That bet goes down, somewhere on the godforsaken fields of Eastern Europe.

◆ ◆ ◆

That evening in Scraggs, Niall Byrne finds out that Tony is still alive.

There is a regular customer who happens to work at the headquarters of Paddy Power, and he says he has some knowledge of the account of Tony 10. He is not speaking on behalf of the organisation, just for himself, because he feels it's the right thing to do. He and Niall step out into the alley and he lays it out for him: Tony is still alive, because they can see from his online account that he is still gambling.

As Niall absorbs this news, which is good in its bizarre way, his informant goes into more detail. Not only is Tony 10 still gambling, for a long time he has been gambling on a scale far greater than Niall Byrne or anyone else who is known to him could even begin to imagine. It will eventually emerge that when Tony was betting these astronomical amounts, Paddy Power staff went looking for a picture of his house on Google Maps. When they found nothing but the modest home in Sandhills, they decided that he must have 'won the Lotto or got an inheritance'.

Now this Paddy Power employee is finally giving Niall a clear idea of the size of the problem Tony 10 has been hiding for so long. The amounts of money involved will later be described by Gardaí to Tony O'Reilly Senior in two shattering words: not repayable.

The next morning Niall goes to see Fiona. Her parents have come to Sandhills to be with her, but for the information he is about to share, Niall asks her to come out and sit with him in the car. He tells her what he knows, that there was no tiger kidnapping, that Tony is alive, but that his gambling debts are enormous. Not repayable.

Looking out the window of the house, Fiona's mother and father are convinced by her reaction that Niall is telling her they have found Tony's body. This is when it all hits her, all the emotions she's been through, the shock, the desperate worry, the anger, the grief, and back again to pleading for reassurance: will he be all right?

The way Niall sees it, when he sat with Fiona in the car, telling her the truth, it was like her life just flipped, like an omelette on a pan. Bang. Upside-down. Sandra O'Reilly says that to see this young woman with a young child, after all she'd been through, realising what had actually happened, was just heartbreaking.

This disaster had been building for months, for years, and the first Fiona knew of it was on this day, when it hit her full force. When there was nothing she could do about it.

◆ ◆ ◆

For Tony 10, any sense that he is on some kind of an otherworldly holiday is now blasted away by the panic of the gambler, one who has lost nearly everything, but who is holding a docket that, if cashed, will enable him to keep betting. But if it is cashed, it may also place him in great danger.

He is contemplating having a couple of pints of Heineken in the hotel bar, longing just to stay here all night, in the atmosphere which feels like that of a tavern – not modern, not antique, just old enough to make him feel comfortable. But he can't stay here all night. He has a decision to make, and he makes it. It is the only one that for him is conceivable. He will drive into Belfast and he will find a Paddy Power office and he will cash that docket. But it is getting late. And he doesn't really know where he is going.

His urge to gamble is still so big, it almost seems to be powering the car back towards Belfast, its driver telling himself that he needs to start betting again, needs to get going. He drives into a multi-storey car park near the centre of the city and gets out of the car, with no idea in his head except to find a random branch of Paddy Power before it closes. It is now after 8.30 p.m., and he expects the offices will be closed at about 9.00 p.m.

He finds an office just around the corner from the car park. It seems like a stroke of good luck, though he can hardly tell the difference any more between good luck and bad luck. He doesn't care, he just wants to keep gambling.

He approaches the manager behind the counter and presents him with the docket. The office is busy with punters looking at the evening racing. Tony 10 is highly agitated, but trying keep a lid on it. The Paddy Power manager is under a lot of strain too, trying to cope with the ramifications of this extraordinary docket that has been handed to him while he is still taking bets on the last races of the day.

The manager starts talking in a distracted way about the currency differences, telling Tony 10 that he could lose €1,500 if he cashes it in here. Tony 10 tells him that is fine, just stick it on his online account. He mentions something about being on his way over to England and staying in Carrickfergus, which he realises straightaway is probably a mistake, but then he is desperate to provide some credible reason for his arrival out of nowhere with a docket for ten grand.

'Bear with me,' the manager says, still taking bets from other punters and paying them out. He indicates that he is going to take the docket to the back office to sort it out, which doesn't feel right to Tony 10. Muttering something to the manager about needing to check his car, he leaves the office. At the corner he stops, gathering his wits, making an effort to compose himself.

As he stands there, a police car comes tearing down the street. It stops outside the bookies. So this is it, he thinks. They have found him. He wants to run, but he just can't bring himself to move. The fear that is urging him to escape is also somehow stopping him.

Then he sees the police car pulling away from the office. He realises they haven't found him at all. He will learn that, by an absurd coincidence, a hit-and-run accident has taken place near the bookies, and that is why the police are here.

In a virtually deranged state, he returns to Paddy Power, to be told by the manager that he just can't get it sorted right now – too busy, too late, and all that stuff that Tony 10 just doesn't want to hear. He is distraught for so many reasons, but for one reason above all – the fact that tonight, there will be no gambling for him. When he gets back to the hotel, defeated, he opens an email from Fiona. He is so disconnected from the places and the people he has left behind, it's like in the back of his mind he's reserving the option of ending all this insanity, of ending his life in this lonely place. And if it comes to that, he doesn't want to be connecting with anyone who might want to stop him. Yet some better instinct rises within him now, urging him to make some sort of contact, to do the right thing, regardless of the outcome. He sends her a text, to say that he is alive, he is OK.

He doesn't realise that he has inadvertently made this known already, that when the Paddy Power manager checked with his colleague in Gorey about this extraordinary docket, the word was passed quickly to the Gardaí in Gorey. Nor does he know that word will be passed from there to his family that he is no longer a missing person. They are told this by the Garda sergeant when they visit the station on the Friday afternoon. They are shown a picture of him taken by the CCTV camera outside a Paddy Power office in Belfast. And while they are only shown the picture for a few moments, Tony O'Reilly Senior notices a detail about the picture, the fact that there are cobblestones outside the office.

Friday morning in Carrickfergus, in view of the fact that 'Niall Byrne' will be extending his stay in lovely County Antrim, he is moved to a different room in Dobbins Inn. Then he heads out for the day, like any other holiday-maker. He is most certainly not like any other holiday-maker in that the first thing he does is check again to see if his story has hit the papers yet. It hasn't. He can't quite decide if this is the calm after all the chaos that has happened, or the calm before the chaos that is to come, but in a severely twisted way it is some kind of calm.

He couldn't get that docket cashed, and he figures he has revealed too much in trying to get it cashed. Regardless of his cravings, he knows that he can't go back there. He feels it would be like walking into the local police station and giving himself up. He is not quite ready for that yet.

Indeed he still can't quite believe what happened outside the betting office, with the arrival of the police car which he was sure was looking for him, but was only passing through on its way to some other emergency. All he knows is that the whole encounter scared the hell out of him, and his nerves could hardly stand a return to that scene.

He still has that walking-around money, which he can use for punting in Ladbrokes and other betting offices in the town. He is doing well, too, on the horses and the dogs and the virtual horses and the virtual dogs, finding himself with what, in any normal circumstances, might be regarded as a decent enough fistful of cash, but which to him is virtually meaningless – just a few quid to play with. Otherwise it seems that he is entirely beaten, and while his normal instinct would be to escape, in some strange way he feels that this is already an escape of sorts, this bubble he has found in Carrickfergus.

He buys a pair of shoes and a pair of jeans to go with them, partly because he wants to, partly because it's the sort of thing they do in films when they're on the run. The only way he can make any sense of what is happening is to pretend that this is a film in which he is appearing as himself. He goes into a tattoo parlour, which is something they probably don't do in films. He didn't mean to get a tattoo, he was just passing a tattoo parlour and the thought occurred to him that he might push in a bit of time here, getting an old tattoo of his fixed, and getting another one done.

Something about the atmosphere of the tattoo parlour gives him a sense that he is entering a sanctuary of sorts, that these guys are operating outside of the normal rules. Here is another parallel world in which he can keep his head down for a while, postponing the inevitable. He gets an old Chinese tribal tattoo covered up, as if rejecting everything in the past, trying literally to cover it over. On his left arm he has inked the name Hailey. Because she will be the future.

The shape of that future is now being determined by events over which he has no control. He pushes in the rest of the afternoon in Ladbrokes, backing horses and dogs with cash, the big stuff all gone down on the laptop back at the hotel, nothing left for him now but the small stuff.

In the hotel bar that evening he finds another form of escapism, drinking at the bar next to a local man who is a Rangers fan. He knows this because the man has the Rangers crest tattooed on the side of his head. As they get friendlier, talking in particular of Alex Higgins, who was apparently well-known to the Rangers fan, it turns out that Tony's drinking companion is 'a recovering alcoholic', his recovery apparently put on hold for this evening at least.

He gives Tony some advice on where to go, and where not to go, in Northern Ireland at this time of year, with his southern accent and southern registration.

Tony explains who 'Hailey' is, that this new tattoo of his has been done for his daughter, but he does not tell his companion of a more grandiose and moving vision which now visits him. He imagines that when they discover him up here, they will somehow have brought Hailey with them, and they will allow him to visit the Giant's Causeway with her, to do this last thing together before he walks into some police station, and possibly out of her life.

◆ ◆ ◆

Though they are being discouraged by the Gardaí from pursuing their own investigations, the extended O'Reilly family gathers on Friday night in Fiona's family home to consider their options. They know that the police would prefer if they just did nothing, but they can't do nothing. Especially now that they know Tony is still alive, but that there are many reasons why he might wish to be dead.

They have seen that picture of him outside the betting office in Belfast, the one they were shown in the Garda station for a few seconds, during which Tony Senior made a mental note of the cobblestones. Using Google Earth, Tony O'Reilly Senior searches for the various Paddy Power offices in Belfast, and finds the only one with cobblestones outside it. They decide that they must go up there, that they need to be somewhere nearer to Tony, or to where he has been, that they may not find him there, but that it's a lot better than waiting in Carlow for a call from the police. At 6.00 a.m. on Saturday, Fiona and Tony's sister Sandra and her husband Colm set out from Carlow to Belfast. By noon, Tony Senior and Niall Byrne will also be on the road north. It is the best place for them to be in every respect, given that the press are now onto the story and are looking in particular for Tony Senior, who is not taking any of their calls.

When the journalists go into Tony's 'local', the front bar of Scraggs, Tony's friends and acquaintances are on alert, thwarting the media or anyone else unknown to them by avoiding all talk of what is the biggest story to come out of Carlow for a long time. Some of the country's leading crime reporters, the sort who would normally be covering gangland slayings and the like, are in town, wanting to talk to anyone who knows anything, their desire sharpened by the unfortunate fact that not only is this an astonishing story in itself, but that for several days nothing else of any consequence seems to be happening in Ireland.

◆ ◆ ◆

In Carrickfergus, when Tony 10 arrives into the betting office on Saturday morning – because that is all he can think of doing – he opens a copy of *The Star* to find that on page 2 there is a picture of Gorey post office. There is the story. The figure of €1.7 million is mentioned, there are lines about his family and friends 'looking for him in the Wicklow mountains'.

He tries to take it all in, devouring it in a few frantic seconds. Until now, the experience of seeing his name in the paper has been confined to the odd report in the *Carlow Nationalist* of some junior football match with Stretford United. He needs to sit down.

He sits on a high stool facing the wall, which is covered in the racing pages, staring down at this page in *The Star*. He reads through the story again, one more time, and then another, just to let it settle in his head. It's not like he wasn't expecting this, but it's still some kind of a shock to see it laid out there in a national newspaper, to see this particular dread becoming a stone cold fact.

The picture of the post office alone sets him off on a wave of regret, for all that went on in there, for what he has squandered. For the fact that he had been really good at something, and still wanted something more. The mention of the €1.7 million leaves him in no doubt that he is well and truly screwed. The image of the family and friends looking for him in the Wicklow mountains is something he can't quite deal with, being one of those things he would normally be reading in the paper about someone else, never imagining that a day might come when they'd be looking for him. And that he'd be reading about it in a newspaper, as he is now, his head spinning in these crazy circles.

There is no picture of him along with the story, which is the one merciful release. He can sit here in the betting office without the fear that someone will recognise him from *The Star*, although he is alert anyway to the demeanour of anyone who comes in the door. Indeed, as he furtively studies the movements of his fellow punters, he starts to wonder how much trouble they might be in themselves, these characters sauntering in for their Saturday bet, giving off these vibes of normality. Then again, he figures there are very few men in any betting office in Northern Ireland, or indeed in the entire world, who are in as much trouble as he is today.

So he regards them instead with a kind of envy, longing for their apparently quiet lives, reminding him of the night in Ardkeen Hospital when Hailey was born, and he saw that man who had also just become a father walking across the car park in the early hours of the morning. He had wished he was that man, had wished he was anyone but the man he had turned out to be.

He starts betting. He is just throwing the money across the counter really, like he wants to be rid of it, this toxic substance, so that it can cause him no more grief. His last bet, with his last £100, is on a horse called *Badea* in the 1.50 p.m. at Beverly, a race with the rather convoluted title of the Award Winning Coachman Caravans Median Auction Maiden Stakes (Class 6), over a distance of seven furlongs.

He has £100 sterling on *Badea* at 11/4. It finishes second.

Back at the hotel, he closes the curtains in his room. He lies on the bed, broken. He is literally and in every other way in a dark place. He just keeps saying, 'fuck … fuck … fuck …' He is no longer just subconsciously reserving that option of ending his life, he is contemplating it. And although he is so full of self-loathing, it seems there is a part of him that will not allow him that release. Somehow he knows he's not going to do it, though in the circumstances it has an obvious attraction.

The women's final at Wimbledon is on the television. Maria Sharapova is playing Petra Kvitová. Though Sharapova is the favourite, he has a feeling that Kvitová might win and he would back her if he could, which he can't. Knowing this, he knows that she will win, which she does.

Lying on the bed, he sees that the tattoo job was not the best. The ink from his arm is running onto the sheets. He can do nothing about it.

He becomes transfixed by it for a while, by these white sheets blackened by the ink, sending this odd echo through his head of the old song 'Carrickfergus', the line about a marble stone, 'as black as ink'. He is transfixed by the new tattoo, by the name Hailey, by the possibility that it is this and nothing else for which he wants to live. That the only thing keeping him here on this Earth is the thought of her going to sleep in his arms listening to 'Living' by Moby, listening to their song.

◆ ◆ ◆

Sandra O'Reilly, her husband Colm, Fiona and her father have found the place they were looking for – the Paddy Power office in Belfast with the cobblestones. They also find the man they're looking for, the one in Paddy Power who remembers dealing with this punter from last night, who is trying to be discreet, but who is clearly sympathetic towards them. Indeed, in their various visits to hotels and betting offices on this day, they will remember those who showed some compassion, and those who mainly seemed to find it amusing that they were looking for someone called Tony O'Reilly, but not the tycoon.

The man in the Paddy Power office recalls that the punter from last night mentioned something about Carrickfergus. And something about wanting to go to England.

They head for Carrickfergus, the four of them, all the while on this nerve-shredding journey, wondering if they will get there too late. They send the word down the line to Tony Senior and Niall Byrne, who have now reached Dublin, and to other friends who are on the way from Carlow.

When they arrive in Carrickfergus, Sandra immediately sees her old Volkswagen Polo in the car park on the waterfront. She feels this enormous sense of relief, and yet it also looks like a classic image of the car abandoned by a person who has committed suicide. But Tony 10 has not committed suicide, he is still lying on his hotel bed in the darkened room, on the sheets blackened by the ink of the tattoo.

They know that he has not committed suicide because he is sending more emails to Fiona. But the nature of these emails is telling them that they need to find him pretty soon. *'I'm very, very sorry'* … *'You'd be better off without me'* … *'Boo Boo* [Hailey] *will be better off with you, tell her I love her.'*

He does not know that Fiona is very near, that she is sitting on a kerb in Carrickfergus crying, convinced now that they are going to find him too late. They contact the local PSNI, and with mounting dread they keep asking if anyone in the betting offices or hotels has encountered this Tony O'Reilly, later cursing themselves that it never occurred to them that he would be pulling the old gag of checking in under the name Niall Byrne.

Accompanied by two young PSNI officers, the search is now becoming more focused. But in Dobbins Inn, Tony 10 is unaware of all this action in his vicinity – until he receives a call from reception saying that the housekeeper is wondering if he wants to have the room cleaned.

It is five o'clock in the evening. Tony knows that in all likelihood no housekeeper would be doing any cleaning at this time. He opens the window of his room and looks out onto the street. He looks to the left, and he sees nobody. If he had looked to the right, he would have seen something different. He would have seen people well known to him.

Thirty seconds later there is a knock on the door. He opens it to find two PSNI officers, one of whom says, 'we are concerned'. Tony sees that both of them have guns, but they are not holding them, or pointing them at him. They are just 'concerned'.

Tony goes back to the bed and collapses onto it. He finds that he is weeping, and that he can't stop. Soon they will let Fiona in to see him, but for now one of the officers closes the door and stays standing in the room, just inside the door, against the radiator. The other one goes downstairs to tell everyone, 'we've found him, we've found him'.

For some time, Tony is on that bed, weeping. For some time, he and the PSNI officer are the only people in the room, while the rest of them stay downstairs, knowing that now they have found him, no more damage can be done. He asks the PSNI officer about who is downstairs – who has come … is Hailey there? Where is she?

He recalls that the PSNI officer was very understanding. That, like a good counsellor, he listened rather than offering a judgement on the situation. He listened for what felt like an hour as Tony poured out all the trouble, all the grief that he'd been carrying around for so long.

Tony recalls that somewhere at the back of all this overpowering sadness, he was starting to get this feeling that was more powerful still, a feeling of relief.

CHAPTER 17

On the drive home from Carrickfergus, at an Applegreen station in Dundalk, he catches a glimpse of an *Evening Herald*. Tony O'Reilly is making the front pages. He is being driven by his sister Sandra and her husband Colm, after a meal and a few pints in a restaurant overlooking the sea in Carrickfergus. To an outsider it must have looked like an extended family gathering, this party of people from the south just quietly eating and drinking and chatting, the drama of the day already done.

For the players in that drama, the mood was somewhat similar to that of a funeral after the initial sadness has lifted and people are trying to reconnect with more regular emotions. The outsider would not have seen Niall in his car across from Dobbins, on the phone to friends in Carlow, telling them that Tony had been found. The outsider would not have seen Niall being joined in the car by Tony, the two of them embracing and breaking down at the enormity of it all.

Sandra recalls that after the trauma they had all been through, in some strange way the meal felt like this lovely get-together, which was yet so bittersweet.

When they reach the family home in Carlow, there is no warmth in the welcome Tony receives from his mother, no open arms, nothing but a look of pure disappointment. It is a look that will continue to burn him for the rest of his life. Perhaps she was feeling a particular sense of betrayal because she had literally contributed to his gambling with that loan of €8,000, which he had punted away like all the other loans. Certainly after the weird sense of relief he had felt when they had finally found him in Dobbins Inn, the feeling of gratitude that at least it was all over now, that look reminded Tony that any such relief was going to be temporary, in fact it was ending already.

In these early days, with the story still making the papers, there is a formal introduction to An Garda Síochána, who will be playing a significant part in his life for some time to come. He is interviewed by two detectives in the house in Carlow of his solicitor John O'Sullivan, an old friend of the family who had joined the search party that went to Carrickfergus. There is nothing of a contentious nature about the meeting, Tony gives a statement admitting everything, stating that it was all his doing, and that there was nobody else involved. He surrenders his passport.

The mood is civil, and they are having cups of tea. Tony is getting the impression that the detectives have an understanding of the broader issues, that, like the PSNI officers, they are not without empathy. He has given them enough information to keep them going – he will be seeing them again soon.

It is felt that for now, the best place for Tony to stay is Fiona's family's home, a bungalow outside Carlow, where he might be able to avoid the reporters. And where he can also make an apology, for what it's worth, to Fiona's family. Sure enough, the reporters don't make it out there, though they've been following his father around Carlow or coming into Scraggs to talk to anyone who might know anything. Indeed, a friend of Tony's is offered ten grand to share his insights with a tabloid paper, an offer he refuses.

When the detectives come to the bungalow to interview him again, there are five of them, with three search warrants, but, like before, Tony won't be giving them any trouble. They conduct the interview in the room in which Tony is staying, Fiona's niece's room, a kid's bedroom. In the telling of his story Tony breaks down several times. The detectives are in no doubt about the sincerity of his remorse.

A few days later he returns to Sandhills. He is spending more time with the detectives, who are eager to find out if he really blew everything on gambling, or if he might still have some of it stashed away. It's a reasonable question, given that it was such a colossal amount of money. But it is clear that there are no signs of extravagance at all in Sandhills. It is the ordinary home of a couple with ordinary incomes. There are no secret ledgers in which Tony 10 was recording his activities. It looks like he really did divert those funds from An Post straight to Paddy Power.

They are interested in his perfectly stacked materials in the spare room, the books and CDs and DVDs, but are satisfied there is nothing criminal in nature here, just an unacceptable level of neatness.

An Post, not surprisingly, have suspended him without pay and are conducting an internal investigation into how he managed to steal €1.75 million from them. They send him a solicitor's letter, asking him to come in for meetings, but he is determined to get into some kind of a treatment programme before engaging with them.

Again there is a sense of unreality to these days, a new kind of unreality, a sense that he is still in shock, that whatever procedures need to be gone through with the authorities, the main thing now is to get himself into treatment. And indeed the authorities are accepting of this too, they agree that he needs to get into some kind of rehabilitation programme and after that, the law will do whatever it does. They can see that he knows he has done wrong, and that there have to be consequences. But also that he has been utterly lost in addiction. And so the main thing to work out now is where he can go for help, and how quickly he can get there.

Calls are made to various well-known treatment centres, advice is sought from counsellors, there are issues about whether Tony's health insurance would cover treatment for gambling addiction, there's a trip to a psychiatric unit in Kilkenny to assess the risk of suicide. There is a random-ness to all of this, they are hoping for the best solution.

Somehow, life as other people know it, that distant dream, is still happening around him. He has to involve himself in it too, looking after Hailey during the day while Fiona is at work. It is not easy in the best of circumstances for anyone to be on their own looking after a ten-month-old child all day, and for a man reflecting on the catastrophe he has brought on himself and his family, it is far less easy. He has no idea how things are going to work out with Fiona, or if they are going to work out, they are both shattered.

In the evenings he leaves the house to walk Jack through the familiar grounds of the college. Conscious that he might meet people he doesn't want to meet, he wears the Nike Mercurial baseball cap he bought in Dundalk, and he doesn't shave. Tony O'Reilly is now taking the same evasive action Tony 10 took when he was on the run.

There is some clarity starting to emerge about treatment, however. Cuan Mhuire, the famous old establishment outside Athy, mainly treats alcoholics, but it expresses a willingness to accept Tony, if he observes the usual conditions. It is a system of self-referral: he must ring them every day, to show his commitment and to see when a bed might be available. The financial terms are the same for everyone. Most of the clients are on social welfare, from which €140 is deducted each week.

After ten days of calling, on 22 July 2011 he enters Cuan Mhuire. He spends the morning of his departure with Fiona and Hailey, before the difficult goodbyes around noon. The last thing he does before leaving the house is to sit in a kind of a daze watching the Tour de France, until he realises he is watching a recording from the previous day. Though it has been a hellish time looking for a place of refuge, it has been lightened occasionally by such a moment of twisted humour.

And by this one, too. After a consultation with a psychiatrist in Dublin, in which Tony tells as much of the story as he can recall, leaving nothing out if he can manage it, he is sitting in the car with his father, pondering the professional assessment. He found the consultation excellent, the psychiatrist clearly absorbed by his story. Now in the car, Tony is looking at a written note, reading out the line at the end of it in which the psychiatrist sets out his conclusion: 'Tony O'Reilly is a pathological gambler.'

Tony turns to his father and he finds himself laughing. 'No shit, Sherlock'.

PART 3

CHAPTER 18

As I approached the entrance of Cuan Mhuire, Athy at 3.45 p.m. on Friday, 22 July 2011, I wondered to myself how I got to this point in my life. I was about to enter a treatment centre for addiction for the next twelve weeks. I had been here once before, but just to visit a friend who is a recovering alcoholic and who had completed the programme last December. Even though I had chatted to him briefly, I had no idea what was ahead of me or how the programme would help me. I didn't know what to expect or what would be expected of me.

As we drove up to the side entrance I thought of the carnage I have caused with my gambling. I have done things that I would never have done in my wildest dreams to fuel my addiction. I have lied to family and friends for years to hide my illness. It had become insidious in every aspect of my life. For me my addiction and my gambling became more important than anything else in my life, more important than eating, sleeping, my health, my marriage, even the birth of my daughter. It dominated my day from the moment I got up to the time I eventually got asleep at night. I could not think straight but I managed to carry my secret with me for years without anyone knowing. I had put myself through weeks, months and years of extreme stress, worry and anxiety and now my family and friends were experiencing the same feelings and fears that have haunted me and that will probably continue to haunt me for years to come.

I felt at this point that I had lost everything, including countless money and my job. I have lost the trust of loved ones, but mainly I felt that I had lost my sanity and my mind. My head was like a roulette wheel spinning spinning spinning but never coming to a stop.

I arrived at the side entrance where the admissions are taken in. There are men in pyjamas waiting to get through a locked door … Why didn't I stop when I was ahead? … My father is with me, putting up a brave face, reassuring me that everything is going to be OK … Why didn't that team just hold to that one-goal lead for five minutes more and give me the big win that I craved and needed to get me back to the point where I got the buzz from gambling? … The door is opened and I am greeted by the nurse … How is my wife going to manage for three months without me? … In fact, how are we going to manage with all the crippling debts? … What are people saying about me behind my back?

My head is like the spin-drier now, spinning faster – faster – faster.

How do I stop the madness in my head? How do I stop the headaches? How do I slow everything down? How do I beat this? How do I get better? Why are people in pyjamas? Surely I won't be asked to do the same! How do I get out of here? How can I turn back the clock?

There must be an easier way.

I am now standing beside a plaque on the wall that reads: 'Cuan Mhuire, a place where I change myself and nobody else.'

I want to change everything, I want answers, I want to be better, I want to be finished with the programme, I want the quick fix like all gamblers do, I want it now.

My mind is still racing as thoughts of bets, scenarios, fears, shame, guilt and worry come flooding into my head. The gambler juggles dozens of thoughts in his/her mind at any one time.

Bang-Click the door is closed and locked behind me, it's now flight or fight time. For a moment my head stops spinning. I focus myself, my thoughts, take a deep breath, decide to accept that I have this problem, this illness, this gambling addiction … I decide to Fight.

Fight my addiction and all the negative thoughts. With that my journey starts on my road to recovery. I walk towards the nurses' station and my head is again full of a dozen thoughts, the main ones being how did it come to this … I am so sorry … I am so sorry …

The nurse meets me in the men's sitting room in the Detox area and checks me in. She tries and succeeds to make me feel at ease, I must look horrified and nervous. I haven't shaven for weeks and have been wearing a baseball hat anytime that I have ventured out of the safe haven that is my house. The embarrassment and guilt that I feel is almost unbearable and such is the enormity of the lengths that I went to in order to obtain money for gambling that I feel I can never face anyone that I know ever again. I can barely look at myself in the mirror.

The Unit man then shows me to my bed, which is one of twelve beds in a separate room that resembles a hospital ward. He then checks my bags for any electrical equipment, papers, etc., which are not allowed in the house. I am then asked to change into a pyjamas which is provided (a lovely paisley one).

I look around and see men that are underweight, weak and visibly sick. There are a few just lying in bed sleeping or reading, the rest are out smoking or comparing drinking stories in the sitting room. I think to myself, I am not like any of these people, I am here for gambling. I am not sick; I just need time to sort out my head.

But the harsh reality hits me, I was sick, I probably looked a lot worse than a lot of the people there without realising it. I was bloated with stress and had put on a lot of weight from eating badly. I had black rings and bags under my eyes from lack of sleep and I felt exhausted and probably looked worse than I felt. I had been physically sick from anxiety attacks brought on from losing bets and from the bad situations I constantly found myself in. This was all due to my out-of-control gambling. Occasionally I experienced severe weight loss from a lack of eating and I had broken out in rashes numerous times. I had constant headaches and experienced constant pressure in my head, a pressure that I can best describe as how it would feel if someone placed their hands on the top of your head and squeezed, sometimes hard and sometimes not so hard, but always squeezing.

But worse than all the physical symptoms of my disease is how my head was. To this day I believe that in the latter stages of my gambling addiction I lost control of my mind and my ability to rationalise and think straight.

I was living in a parallel world to the real nightmare I was living. In this world I could justify what I was doing and I felt that I would always get that big win that would get me back to the time when I was ahead, back to the initial buzz. In this world everything was OK, I felt safe and could gamble freely without fear of the consequences that I would inevitably and eventually have to face. I could block out all the bad and cocoon myself away from all my problems both financial and personal.

When I talk to family and friends they ask me how I didn't crack and slide over the edge. To this day I really don't know, but I do feel that the times when I was at the bottom of the hole I had dug for myself, I felt suffocated, isolated and could see no way out, no glimmer of light above. The harder I tried to dig myself out and get back money to the people and places from whom and where I had borrowed or stole from to fuel my addiction and my nightmare, the deeper I got into everything and the further I found myself from salvation.

My first few days in Cuan Mhuire were mainly spent in bed either sleeping or reading. I suffered with constant pounding headaches and my mind was racing full of fear, worry and anxiety. I started reading *The Gambler*, a book written by Oisin McConville. I had rushed around for days trying to buy it in shops and online, thinking that it would have all the answers (a typical trait of a gambler, wanting all the answers, wanting them now, wanting the easy way). I finally got it and when I started reading it I realised that it was mainly about his football career and only had a small bit in it about gambling. I would have to do it all myself, the hard way, the proper way. I realised that I would have to slow everything down, be patient and work through everything myself.

I spent a lot of time reflecting on the last number of years. I thought about the bets I had placed, the money I had won and subsequently lost. I tried in vain to count up the vast amounts of money I had squandered on gambling. I thought a lot about the losing bets, the last-minute goals and the horses falling at the last. I remember waiting on bets where the long odds on shots would somehow inconceivably lose and cost me the big accumulator that would have 'got me back'. Even if this had happened I would have started the whole crazy cycle all over again. Looking back now, I can see the madness of the whole thing, but while in the grips of my addiction I was blinded to everything else other than gambling.

Nothing else mattered, I fretted to get that first bet on in the morning, every morning. I can relate to how a drug addict or alcoholic must feel when they wake and instantly want their fix just to function, just to feel right. I just needed to place a bet and it didn't matter if it won or lost, I just needed to place it. I used to stay up into the early hours most nights gambling online and sometimes I wouldn't sleep for days. I would have blackouts and wake in the middle of the night in a pool of sweat with thoughts of nothing else other than gambling. I would set my alarm to get up during the night to check results and ongoing bets. I eventually started staying in the spare room so my wife wouldn't notice my erratic behaviour, using our newborn baby as an excuse. I would use any excuse so I could gamble when and where I wanted without question or interruption …

CHAPTER 19

The journal that Tony O'Reilly started on the day he entered Cuan Mhuire would eventually fill several hardback notebooks, each entry usually written at the end of a day, capturing his authentic reactions to whatever was happening in this other world he had entered, the world of Recovery. The journals are a kind of a middle world, where he can try to understand how he got to this place, and try to prepare somehow for the rest of his life, which may promise many things, but will almost certainly include a spell in jail.

Like everything he does, from the start he throws himself into it wholeheartedly, which is a very positive trait in most circumstances, but which can work against you in a big way if you happen to develop a dangerous addiction.

It must be emphasised that these are the words of Tony O'Reilly, not Tony 10, that it is his voice and not the voice of the gambler that is struggling to emerge here, starting to find itself again. In these journals, sometimes written in the saddest of circumstances, he seems to be trying to retrieve some part of his soul that had been given over to the madness of Tony 10, and trying to deal with the consequences of that vast aberration.

As is his wont, the handwriting is perfectly clear, there is hardly a word crossed out or a line revised, there is no 'editing' of his feelings, though of course the excerpts here are distilled from the original, a collection of moments reflecting the overall experience of these twelve weeks.

Usually he would write two pages at a time, in about twenty minutes, or whatever amount of time his new timetable would permit. Indeed, one of the first entries is a neatly laid-out version of that timetable for the Detox Unit, so very different from the daily schedule of racing and football that had so recently consumed his days.

RESIDENTS – PLEASE TAKE NOTE OF THE FOLLOWING TIMETABLE
SECOND WEEK MEETINGS BEGIN WHEN YOU ARE DETOXED AND WHEN YOU ARE READY TO START A MEETING

1st and 2nd Week

Meditation in Room 16	8 a.m.
Breakfast	9 a.m.
Unit Duties	9.30 a.m.–10.30 a.m.
Morning Meeting in Room 26	10.45 a.m.–12.15 p.m.
Lunch	12.30 p.m.–1 p.m.
Break	1 p.m.–1.45 p.m.
Afternoon meeting in Room 26	1.45 p.m.
Tea Break	3 p.m.
Mass (Main Assembly Hall)	
Meditation (following Mass)	5 p.m.
Dinner	6 p.m.
Rosary	8 p.m.
Bed	11 p.m.

SATURDAY

Breakfast 8.30 a.m.
Mass 11.30 a.m.
Dinner 1 p.m.
Tea 5.30 p.m.

SUNDAY

Breakfast 8.30 a.m.
Meditation 11 a.m.
Mass 12 p.m.
Dinner 1 p.m.
Tea 5.30 p.m.

Friday, 22 July 2011

… I had to hand up all my clothes and belongings. I was allowed to keep my books and writing equipment, and my iPod and radio which weren't technically allowed because they were electrical. I had to hand up my chargers, but seeing the horror on my face at not having my iPod, they let me charge it on the QT for a couple of hours.

The room is divided in two, six beds in each, one locker and one chair each. I met John in bed 5, Ollie in bed 6 and John in bed 9. John 9 was the first person I really talked to, but within an hour or so had met and chatted to most of the lads. John 5 seemed a bit quiet, I think he is like me, he susses people out first before engaging fully with them. In this place however I have no choice. I slept through meditation and went for fish & chips and missed the Rosary at 8. Stayed in bed for the rest of the night, chopping and changing between books, chat radio, and listening to music on my iPod. Richard in bed 4 arrived in around 10.30 and livened the place up. Good character (snores more than me), chatted till about 12 swapping stories, then lay awake for hours amidst choruses of snores before finally falling asleep around 4 – what an eye-opener today has been. Fell asleep listening to 'Living' by Moby, me and Hailey's song – miss her so much. X

Saturday, 23 July

Every morning you have to ensure that your locker is clear and that the floral pattern on your duvet is facing upwards. You cannot lie on the duvet or the flowery pillow case and you have to ensure that the bed is dressed at all times in case of spot checks. They told me that I would be getting my clothes back on Sunday so that was a bit of good news. My sister Louise dropped over slippers and new pyjamas and writing material. I also found out I could make phone calls and because I have my clothes back will be allowed to have visitors on Sunday, meaning I will see Fiona and Hailey. That really cheered me up. I don't know if I could have gone a week without seeing them.

You only realise how much you miss the ones you love when you can't see them. … Detox don't have to go to meditation so I spent a lot of the day in bed reading my Paul Merson book [*How Not to be a Professional Footballer*] and talking to the lads in the room. John in bed 5 was the only one who knew about my story. Went to dinner at 6 which was chicken curry (food not too bad), starting to get to know a lot of the lads on the programme, everyone seems to be sound enough. Starting to hear a lot of interesting stories. Still not sleeping too well at night, a lot of things still going on in my head. Guilt, depression, hurt I have caused other people, a sense of 'when am I going to wake up from this dream?'… Richard was moved so the snoring was a little less loud. Had a blinding headache, had to get tablets off the nurse at 6 in the morning.

Sunday, 24 July

I went for my lunch and waited with excitement for my visitors. Fiona, Hailey and John O'Sullivan arrived at about half-three, had a nice afternoon, was great to see them all, had a nice sandwich in the Garden Centre and a good chat. The Boo (Hailey) was still a bit out of sorts but it was still great to see her. Fiona met this client, Richard, and thought he was a doctor, in fairness I would have thought the same if I had not met him before. When they left I went back to bed and missed tea, I was shattered. Ended up taking part in a table quiz which is run by Brian, one of the facilitators, at 9 on a Sunday. It was €1.50 each for a table of four. We got on OK, came second, might have done better if Peter didn't disappear all the time. We all got €3 back for coming second – hope this isn't a form of gambling, well, not the form I was used to doing. Sunday night didn't get a wink of sleep. Tommy was having a bad night (tablets?). He was shouting and roaring in his sleep and woke me up on a number of occasions. Hope I won't be stuck in Detox for another week.

Monday, 25 July

My first real day of the programme started with meditation in Room 16. Wasn't too bad, just relaxing, listening to music, followed by the Serenity Prayer. Breakfast was followed by our daily tasks. I was in the tea-room which was a load of shite because you had to be there four times a day. Had breakfast, then got two bits of good news. I was being moved to room 31, away from Detox, and also I was being changed from the dining room to the Detox bedroom for cleaning, which meant that I only had to clean one time in the morning. I can feel a pattern here, the way I try to hang on to anything positive, any little victory, because I know that soon enough I'll be down again. So I'm happy about having to clean only once in the morning in a place where I'm waiting to go to jail probably, trying to avoid the bigger feeling that I should never have put myself in here in the first place. Moved my stuff up to room 31 to share with the two Johns and Joe. It was like a hotel compared to Detox, warm water, shower and bath and decent beds. Decided to try to stop eating shite and start walking around the perimeter of the complex, three laps, which I'd say is about two miles or 25 minutes walking. I rang Fiona a few times and rang my Da a couple of times. Can't really get the sense of what's happening at home or in the outside world. I know it's been tough on everyone especially Fiona, and even though the meetings tell me to live in the present, it's hard for me to forget the past and especially not to worry about the future. A lot of people when they leave here just have to worry about sobriety, I have to worry about this but also about a lot of things they have already lost, like wives and children. Then there is the financial side of everything. I am worried that it will be me that finally puts the nail in my father and mother's coffin. I miss Fiona and Hailey so much, I will never take anything for granted again. I started crying listening to Leona Lewis' 'Run' on the iPod. Never thought I'd do that, but then I never thought I'd do a lot of things.

Tuesday, 26 July

During the Rosary in the small room last night 'T' tried to rob medication from the nurses' office by trying to fit his arm into the smallest of windows in the glass. We all broke our balls laughing at him. He is so sincere in all the meetings, apologising and thanking them for second chances, then risks it all for a few Librium. We had our second meeting with Pat Shaw facilitating and I spoke at the end for the first time about my addiction, how I was in here for gambling not alcohol – it's the first time I'd say that everyone realised I was in for something different. I rang Fiona a few times today, she seemed a bit down in herself, and started to get a bit upset when I was talking to her. I hope she is OK, she was a bit down yesterday too, which kinda put me in bad form as well. I'm worried that we might not be able to get through everything … I have decided only to ring her once a day for a while, I am getting help in here, she needs space and time to think. She was telling me that when she says 'Where is Daddy?', Hailey looks out the window. I can't describe how much I hate myself when I think of that scene, the guilt is overwhelming. And I am stuck with it in here, I can do nothing about it, the time to do something about it is long gone. If I had been able to tell my father or Niall Byrne about the trouble I was in, back when I wanted to tell them, maybe I could have avoided leaving Hailey with this problem, but I just couldn't do it. And that's how I see myself sometimes, as just a problem for her, a problem she doesn't even know exists at this stage, all she knows is that Daddy should be there and he's not. I have these really dark times in here, when I can see no way back.

Wednesday, 27 July

Woke up in better form than yesterday, done the meditation and listened to the story 'The Precious Present', which in theory was all about living in the present and not looking back at the past or worrying about the future. As I mentioned before this is very hard for me to do. I won't ever be able to forgive myself for what I have put my family through, even though they seem to have forgiven me somewhat. The future looks very bleak, probably jail for God knows how long, no job prospects, probably lose the house, etc. But on the bright side if I have Fiona and Hailey by my side I think I will be able to deal with whatever comes. I just hope they can. The support of family and friends has been brilliant, I will be forever grateful. I feel very lucky in that regard. I think everyone as part of schooling should spend a month in a place like this, to help them realise how much great work gets done by the facilitators and how powerful groups can be when working together with structured rules and guidelines … Enjoyed Mass but was not interested come the Rosary. We did two laps of the grounds four times, one hour in total walking. Can't wait for the gym next week. Did a bit of reading of King Kenny's book [*King Kenny: An Autobiography*] and went to bed about 11.30 p.m. Went asleep thinking about Fiona and Hailey, how I would love to be home even for two minutes just to tuck them in and give them a kiss and cuddle. xxx

Saturday, 30 July

Found out that Ollie had decided to leave. I thought he was a bit down last night when we snuck into the gym to play table tennis and pool, and it wasn't just because I thumped him at pool, all the practice in Gorey doing me good there. A couple of us tried to talk Ollie out of leaving but to no avail. I think some of the lads were a bit harsh on him, trying to play practical jokes, and he overheard them talking about him. Ollie is a quiet chap who takes everything to heart, talking to him for two minutes any gobshite would realise this. Some people eh? Even from the stories told yesterday in the meeting you can pick out the eejits, people who don't take this seriously, the genuine people, the quiet people and the fucked up people like me. I am sad to see Ollie go. I got his number and wished him the best and he genuinely hopes that I get on OK in my case. I liked him, he was liked a lot.

Sunday, 31 July

There was choir practice in the morning, which I really got into. It's the only way to get through the programme, to get into it and get involved in everything.

Was talking to Tony Senior on the phone, he was saying that my story made the papers in England and even in America. My sister and brother-in-law were the first visitors to arrive, then Niall, they have been great since the shit started, well, everyone has been. A lot of people have been asking for me and sending their good wishes. Then Fiona and the Boo Boo arrive shortly afterwards. My heart always skips a beat when I see the black 307 driving in. We all had tea in the coffee shop, having a few laughs, then Sandra, Colm and Niall left. It was drizzling all day but it managed to clear up for about forty-five minutes at 5 p.m., so that me, Fiona and Hailey could go for a walk around the grounds. I really enjoyed this, it's one of the first times in ages that I was truly relaxed. I got probably only my second photo taken with Hailey since she was born. It's disgraceful, I was always paranoid about getting my photo taken because of all the weight that I had put on through stress. It's a lovely photo, I can't wait to get a copy of it. What the fuck have I put everyone through? I am so sorry it hurts. I was crying all the way back to my room, went to bed at 10.30 but didn't sleep till about 4. I had so much running through my head, past, present and future – money, jail, love, hate, regret, Fiona, Hailey, everything … I can't wait to get out of here even though it is helping me. I can't wait to get this court case over with and whatever becomes of it and then start afresh.

Monday, 1 August

In the weekly works meeting where everyone gets their jobs for the week I got the one job that I didn't want, the stupid kitchen. This must be a part of my punishment. When I look back I had a handy job in the post office, how did I fuck it up? Myself, Peter and Richard are in the wash-up area for the week, it is hard work but at least the time goes quickly. I wrote Fiona a letter on my break and bought her a little book on Hope, I hope she likes it. I hope the letter explains a little bit of the power of addiction and how it consumed me. We had our evening meeting with Tim, who is training to be a facilitator, a job I wouldn't mind doing in the future, a counsellor or a facilitator of gambling addicts. I hope everything will be OK, I hate Fiona being unhappy. I wish I knew what I could do to make her day. Maybe I am doing it by being in here, maybe there is nothing I can do, maybe all the damage is done already. Maybe this damage is irreversible. I would murder a pint right now, maybe this is further punishment as well.

Tuesday, 2 August

A chap from Navan was reading yesterday's *Star* and exclaimed in a thick Navan accent: 'Jesus, boy, you are in the paper'. Pat Shaw had told me that there was an article in it alright, it was just the same bullshit that was in the other papers. A fair few of the people in here are starting to twig who I am, and about my story, but the great thing is, I am not being judged or made feel unequal. Everyone in here has had an addiction of some sort – that is what makes the programme work for most people.

Wednesday, 3 August

Still not getting a great night's sleep. I find that when I am talking about my addiction and my story, my mind seems to be overactive and racing when I am trying to sleep. This, coupled with the fact that my mattress has about a dozen springs sticking out of it, makes the few hours in bed restless ones.

But I went to my first GA [Gamblers Anonymous] meeting at 8.30 this evening. Paul spoke first, a young man with a new wife and baby girl, he had lost everything good, and is up to his neck like me in debt. He spoke well and a lot of things he mentioned were similar to me.

Jim was an older gentleman who had gambled away over 400k of his own money. Lar, the other person in the house, said a few words before me. He says that when he was gambling he felt he belonged. He was going out with a girl for seven years but she had to leave after standing by him for three or four treatment centres. She couldn't take it any longer. He hopes to find a way to get back to her in time. I hope he does.

He said he was having problems within his group, that he was in a room with lads that were doing drugs and he asked to be moved without ratting on the other lads. It's a common question in here: 'are you here for yourself or for court?' I guess the lads in his room are just here for court. Me, I know I am here for court purposes, but mainly I am here for myself first and foremost, my family and friends, but also for my sanity. I said a few words at the end of the meeting and uttered the words I never thought I would hear myself say:

'Hello, my name is Tony, I am a compulsive gambler and I have not had a bet today.'

Friday, 5 August

Was talking with John in the room for about two hours about life, where it all went wrong for the two of us and what the fuck were we going to do after we got out of here. There is no real point getting into anything until after the court case, but I am definitely leaning towards a career in counselling. I really feel that this is my calling. I am good with people and think I have the tools to be good at it and to make a difference. Between now and the court case I have decided to make amends, to read and study about counselling, and do a day or two voluntary work here in Cuan Mhuire. I will do what

I did when I dropped out of college and disappointed Ma and Da, I will make people proud of me again. You never know, maybe I will get a job in the place that cured me. I genuinely feel that my reason for being here is to help people. I know it's going to be tough but I will Get There.

Sunday, 7 August

I had a nice hour with Fiona when the other visitors had left. She wrote me a letter which I read when she left. It was hard to read it, but I can't argue with some of the things she was saying or how she felt over the last year or so. After the table quiz I wrote her back a letter in which I tried to explain things to her and how I wouldn't blame her if she had decided to leave or if she decides to leave in the future.

Monday, 8 August

I started my new job today in Detox, this involves checking in and looking after new arrivals. Checking bags, making them feel at home (it is a fairly daunting place to arrive into, especially for gamblers), making sure they all get fed, arrive at meetings on time.

'K' was kicked out today for having a relationship with 'S'. The logic behind 'no relationships' is that apparently if you are sharing your problems on a one-to-one basis, you are less likely to be truly yourself in your meetings. I suppose it makes sense.

Tuesday, 9 August

News of me and my story is slowly filtering throughout the place. I knew it would eventually.

One-to-one counselling is starting next week, I hope I get someone good like Pat or Liam. I have a lot of issues to sort out, I still don't know how I got from being in a great job, good money, to sitting in a rehab centre recovering from a chronic disease that has ripped my world apart. However I am still in a better place mentally than I have been for a long time. Ups and downs, but I think the ups are catching up.

Had a few sausages and stale bread at 10.30 a.m. for my breakfast and got chatting to 'R'. He isn't the worst old devil but tends to annoy people in the house because he is hard to get away from. Why is everyone always in a hurry? There is no rush — there is no rush — there is no rush, as Tom Shanahan the counsellor would say.

I can't help but worry about Fiona trying to organise bills and things. It is a total mess.

Later I just stayed in my room writing letters. I wrote one to Fiona venting my frustration and anger at myself. I will give it to her on Saturday.

I went to bed in bad humour and I could feel the pressure building in my head for the first time in ages. What a dickhead, what a loser I am. Earlier I rang Niall for his birthday, he was on the way into Scraggs for a pint with Martyn. I wished I was there. Later that night I wished I was home with Fiona and Boo, it's the first time I have felt like leaving since I came in here. But hey, I may get used to it.

TIMES AND DUTIES FOR DETOX UNIT

9 a.m.   Call all residents in the Unit for breakfast, seat them at table, make toast, pour out tea at the table. No resident is to walk around with a cup of tea.

9.30 a.m.   Organise people in the Dining Room to clean tables, wash delph, floors, walls, etc., taking care of both refuse containers. Close off Smoking Area and Unit door while cleaning is going on.

                     * Supervise and help to get showers, hand basins and toilets into perfect order.

> * Dust off walls of bathroom, clean walls and skirting boards with a dry duster, wash floors and dry well, paying special attention to cleaning corners properly.

9.40 a.m.   Train residents how to make their beds properly, how to pull out beds from the walls and brush and dust behind them. Remove all items of clothes from chairs, beds, lockers and floor. No bags to be left under the bed.

> The Unit man himself cleans the urinal each morning with steel wool, and washes rubber boundary with deck-scrub brush.

10 a.m.   Check that all other chores, sitting room, glass doors and smoking area are being attended to.

10.40 a.m.   Call all residents for second week's meeting and send them to the appropriate room in time for their meeting.

10.45 a.m.   Tea break.

11 a.m.   Send all residents in Detox Unit for their morning meeting.

11.15 a.m.   Tidy and clean Room 5, wash bathroom, hand basin, toilet, shower and floor.

> * Answer the phone while nurse is engaged with residents, meetings, admissions, etc.
>
> * Ensure that all residents in Detox have a fresh jug of water and tumbler.

12.25 p.m.   See that all residents are in Dining Room for lunch, if anyone is unwell, report to the nurse.

12.30 p.m.   Help serve lunch, get your own lunch, make sure everyone clears off plates, tables, etc., organise clean-up.

1.35 p.m.   Remind everyone on Week 2 about their afternoon meeting. Check all rooms to ensure that residents have returned to work programme.

2 p.m.	Check unit, smoking area, bathrooms, toilet, dining room, sitting room, regarding tidiness and cleanliness.
2.30 p.m.	Check residents to ensure that they are comfortable and not distressed.
3 p.m.	Tea break for residents and yourself. Tidy up and reset for dinner. Report Off Duty.

NO TEA OR COFFEE TO BE MADE IN DINING ROOM OUTSIDE Of MEAL TIMES – EXCEPT WITH THE PERMISSION OF THE NURSE ON DUTY.

DETOX UNIT DUTIES 3 p.m.–11 p.m.

3 p.m.	Report on duty, visit residents in Unit and bring those for 4 p.m. meeting to Sitting Room. Answer phone, etc. for the nurse while she takes the meeting.
3.10 p.m.	Visit bathroom, toilet and shower areas and bedrooms to ensure they are in perfect condition when you take over. Have a chat with anyone in bed who is unable to attend meetings.
4.55 p.m.	Call all residents for Mass and encourage them to be on time. Only one Unit man to remain on duty during Mass and meditation. All others to attend.
6.00 p.m.	Ensure all are seated for dinner and serviced dinners. Have your own dinner with them.
6.20 p.m.	Get everyone to clear plates and organise the wash-up.
6.40 p.m.	Go around the house and ensure all are going to the 7 p.m. meeting.
6.55 p.m.	If you have meeting, ensure that someone is there to relieve you on time.
7.55 p.m.	Ensure all are going to Sitting Room for the Rosary and encourage anyone well enough to kneel down.
8 p.m.	Say the Rosary with the residents in the Sitting Room.
8.20 p.m.	On AA night do a round-up of rooms to ensure all are going to their meetings.

9 p.m.   Tea break in Unit, clean up tables and reset for breakfast.

10 p.m.   Allow residents out for last smoke before bedtime.

10.30p.m.   Call all residents sleeping in Unit and send them to bed. Ensure they lie between the sheets on patterned pillow case. Turn on relaxation music, turn off lights and encourage all to settle for the night. Check bathroom, shower and toilet to ensure it is perfectly clean before handing over to the night man.

* On admission of a resident, record all belongings in book provided, give them PJ's if they have not got their own – keep toiletries, towels and shaving gear in locker. Lock away all other belongings in lock-up, clearly labelled with name and bed number. Fill a jug of fresh water and leave on locker with a tumbler. Encourage the person to drink a lot of water.

* If you have time to spare, sit and chat with residents in Sitting Room or with someone in bed.

* Always inform the nurse if you are leaving the Unit.

11 p.m.   Report off duty.

Wednesday, 10 August

Most of the people in here like to be kept busy to keep their minds off things. I'm different in that I like to spend time alone to reflect on things and get my mind in order. The first thing I had to do in the Detox unit was check on 'P', a sixty-six-year-old former army man who came down from the centre in Galway. It took a while to persuade him to change into his PJ's but when he did he relaxed. He told me that he had served in Cyprus and knew Paphos and the church where me and Fiona got married. I hope we can bring Hailey there some day to visit when she is old enough. He also told me that all he does is get half-a-dozen cans each night and likes watching westerns.

His wife doesn't like drink at all and so sent him in. Maybe I'm being naive, but he doesn't really seem to have a drink problem. There were seven people at the GA meeting, three from the house and four from outside. It was chaired by 'B', who gambled similar amounts to me. He had trials with a few English clubs when he was fifteen, including Crystal Palace and Leeds, but broke his elbow. I guess that's when things started to go wrong for him. Everyone shared and it was interesting. I shared a good bit tonight, basically going through my story from the first bet I can remember until now. It was easy to talk, I am good in groups, but still get the butterflies before I tell my story.

Thursday, 11 August

I went into the Sewing Room and ordered something for Hailey for her birthday and got her one of the Guardian Angel Mirrors from the Garden Centre. It's the most time and effort I've put into a present for a while. It felt good, it was from the heart. I did up a playlist on the iPod and went for a walk. I can't describe what it was, maybe the music, maybe the fine weather, maybe the quiet surroundings, but for a long time I felt as if I was at peace with myself. I walked for about forty-five minutes, doing six laps. I found myself thinking about everything, but mainly having nice thoughts. I was also smiling to myself on numerous occasions ... then this evening at about ten to nine I decided to go down to the church for a bit of quiet time. When I walked into the oratory I can't describe what I felt, but I could feel something in there. I sat and thought and felt tears rolling uncontrollably down my face. This is the moment when I finally forgave myself and decided to move on. I am now starting to look at everything in a positive way. Today hopefully is the turning point in my programme and also in my recovery, but most importantly I think it's the turning point in my life. I think I can face anything thrown at me. All I hope is that Fiona can see this through as well. I think she will.

Saturday, 13 August

Liverpool only drew 1–1 with Sunderland, I was a bit down over that, but hey, there are more important things in life now. It's the first time in a long time that I didn't feel like having a bet on the Saturday soccer. It felt strange but good, however I was still trying to pick out teams that I would have backed. I mustn't be fully cured, maybe I never will be. Pathological gambling is something that you always have, but you have to 'arrest' it, as it says in the handbook.

Sunday, 14 August

Niall brought me over the guitar – I hope to learn a few tunes on it … I saw an ambulance coming and going out of the admissions area, it turned out that 'M' had broken up a razor, sharpened a tea spoon, then locked himself in the shower and slit his wrists and arms. 'R' got him patched up and onto the ambulance. I think he wasn't allowed a visitor and that is what could have sent him off the edge – in hindsight maybe he shouldn't have been here, he was in a bad place mentally. The day before he had been sitting to the left of me in the Introductory meeting, when I heard this sound, tap … tap … tap … coming from him. I looked across and saw that the tap … tap … tap was his tears dropping on the pages he was holding. I guess that should have told us he was even more fragile than the others. But then again he was only doing what some of us want to do, but can't bring ourselves to actually do. I'd say that most days now I have a moment or two when I am overcome by the scale of what I have done, when I feel so low it seems to make perfect sense to go down the road that 'M' has taken. Someone in here trying to kill himself just reminds you that there is a way out of this, that it might not be what you want, but then you've put yourself beyond the point where you're ever going to get what you want anyway. It reminds you how close to the end you might be, how close to it we all are.

'J McE' arrived back on the doorstep looking to get back in. Apparently he had been drinking and living rough in Athy for the last few days. He has been spotted in bus stops drinking cans. I was talking to him and he seemed out of his head. I think he has mental health problems too … went to bed, listened to iPod for a few hours, trying to decide which songs I'd like to learn on guitar, if and when I start to learn it.

Tuesday, 16 August

Early today I was called over to the Old Folks place to change an old man's diaper. We residents help out here because some of the old folks obviously need help with very basic things, and it is good for us too in a way because after the stuff that some of us have done in our addictions, it reminds us of the need for some humility. I went with Gareth, who for some years has had no sense of smell. Which in the situation we are facing, is just incredible. The old man we are helping is incontinent, so we have to take his clothes and the bed sheets and put them in a bag. We try to have a bit of small talk – he says he's originally from Galway – but really we're concentrating on just getting this done. We have to give him a shower and fresh clothes and bed sheets. I won't go too much into it, except to say that every small thing in here changes your view on life, gives you the sort of perspective you never thought would come your way, not in a million years.

Wednesday, 17 August

At the GA meeting I talked about acceptance, forgiveness, humility, change, hope. I was talking to 'A' about becoming a counsellor, and even though it seems a difficult and expensive thing to do, I will find a way because it's not about the money (even though it would be nice to be comfortable), it's about helping people and about the feeling I get when I do this. It is about unconditional love, both feeling it and giving it. It's about rebuilding my life block by block – there will be times when they will tumble but we have to restart and continue to build them again.

Thursday, 18 August

I was changed to a single room yesterday. It's grand, the bed is a lot more comfortable and I slept well even though I was up half the night listening to music. Earlier I bumped into Liz, from housekeeping, on the corridor, and I mentioned Fiona's birthday was coming up, and she told me that Josephine gets lovely cards handmade and the two of them went out of their way to make sure that I had it for Saturday. I am writing this at 12.15 on Friday, I am just after getting the card and it is beautiful. Hopefully Fiona will like it. I will have to think of something nice to put in it. Not a present but some nice words. I rang Niall also and organised a small bunch of flowers. I was talking to John O'Sullivan and he notified me that An Post won't give me my P60 until I contact M O'Loughlin directly. Now they want a statement from me. I wish they would just terminate my contract and let me get on with my recovery. By denying me my P60 they are denying me claiming any welfare, and paying for treatment. I am flat broke and they probably think I have thousands hid away. Afraid not … but I don't blame them, in fact I feel sorry for them, because it can't be any fun for them dealing with all this garbage. They would prefer to be doing almost anything else I'm sure, and it goes to show how many people's lives can be affected for the worse by someone with a gambling addiction – people you never even met … I have heard that Cuan Mhuire sometimes helps with funding for counselling courses, so maybe I will be able to fulfil that dream after all.

Saturday, 20 August

It's Fiona's birthday today. I am writing this at 11.45 p.m. after finishing work and talking to her on the phone. I am fairly depressed at the moment. I had a good start to the day, I watched Liverpool beating Arsenal 2–0 so I was in great form. Fiona arrived with Hailey, we had a nice day. Fiona was in an OK mood but I thought she was a little stand-offish – I don't know, I told myself not to be paranoid. But I honestly think the whole thing is starting to get to her, and I'm in here with my unconditional love and spirituality and Bible, etc. The main thing that's wrong with me is that I went out of my way today to get flowers and especially the card, and I was delighted giving it to Fiona. However when I finally got through to her at 11 p.m., by which time I assumed she would have read it, she was quiet on the phone, which was OK, but she never mentioned the card which was OK as well, I thought she just forgot until just before she got off the phone she mentioned that she had read it. I said, 'Well?', she just said, 'Well what?' I swear it was like she just tore the heart out of me. I asked if she liked it and she just shrugged it off … I know that I have done wrong. I know that I was a bollox for the last year or so when I was stressed up to my eyeballs with everything. I know Fiona is stressed and up to her eyes in worry and shit. I know it's going to be hard – I know that she is finding it hard to understand or to forgive me. I have been so positive for the last week or so, but this has really knocked the stuffing out of me, it really has. Maybe I am living in a dream world in here, that everything is OK and is going to be OK. Slowly everything is changing.

Sunday, 21 August

I wanted to ring to cancel all visits today but decided not to, which is something I am learning to do. While I still cannot control my emotions, I can after a while take a step back and think things through. I decided to ring Fiona at 11 a.m. while I was passing a phone. I'm glad I did – I explained how I felt to her and in turn she explained that while the card was lovely, it was just words and at the moment that is not enough, she needs to see actions. And while she accepts that

I have made changes she still needs to see more. I was delighted she was thinking this way, it shows an understanding as such of where we need to go … Niall arrived today and Paddy and Bianca too. I was happy Paddy arrived, now everyone I would consider a close friend has come over to visit, that means so much. As for Niall, what can I say? These few weeks have really convinced me what a great friend he is, and has been over the years. I know he will stand shoulder to shoulder with me right to the end. That goes for everyone, family and friends like Andy and Martyn. And I know Fiona will be there too, even though at times I wonder why. It was a nice afternoon, Tony Senior arrived with Jack the dog, he has been crying for me all week, he nearly wagged his tail off.

Monday, 22 August

'N' was sitting opposite me at the GA meeting, he gave out about the lack of structure in the meetings, but I think it is lack of structure in him. I rang Fiona afterwards, she was getting stuff ready for MABS [Money Advice and Budgeting Service], she has the statement which I did for An Post, detailing the scale of my gambling, and she was beating herself up for not realising back then that there was a problem. People just don't understand how we addicted gamblers can do it, how we can hide so much. I worry this might be too much for her, the whole thing. I hope not, because I know that when we get all the shit out of the way we will have a good life together. Still I felt bad, guilty and angry. I went to bed in bad humour. I felt the pressure building back up inside me. I got very angry with myself and agitated, I felt like wrecking the room. It's the first time I have felt anger in a while, I didn't sleep much, so much going on in my head. I can get through this but I need my wife and daughter with me – I love them so much.

Saturday, 27 August

I went over to Liam (counsellor) around 10 a.m. to show him my statement to An Post, he got me to read it out to him. He then chatted to me for a little while, which in fact turned into a counselling session. He talked about things years ago – the sugar factory, college, my promotion, and what came out of it all was FEAR mainly, and wanting to prove people wrong. It was a great insight.

When I was leaving his office he gave me two books, *A Million Little Pieces* by James Frey, and a book on the history of the Jesuits.

Sunday, 28 August

It is Hailey's [first] birthday tomorrow and also two months since I was last in Gorey. It's amazing how I have gotten from where I was to where I am now. I have five weeks and five days left in Cuan Mhuire, it seems like a long time but it will probably fly. A few people came over for Hailey's birthday, since I won't see her tomorrow… Can't believe I am in here for her first birthday … Niall was telling me that his daughter Katie, who is my god-daughter, was in a class preparing for Communion. And something came up about the godparents being involved. So Katie put her hand up and asked the teacher, 'what happens if your godfather is going to be in jail?' … It seems that Niall had explained to her as best he could that sometimes when people do bad things, as I did, they have to go to jail. The teacher apologised later to Niall, because she actually knew me, and felt that she should have seen this coming. But there was no need really, this kind of thing happens when there's a mess of this size to be dealt with. All of Carlow knows where I am, I think, I don't care. They're saying: 'You would never guess who's in Cuan Mhuire.' I am famous but for all the wrong reasons … Fiona was telling me that MABS are looking for €100 out of €188, leaving me with €88 euro a week to live on. Not too bad I guess, I can handle that. Maybe if I get a FÁS course I will get a little more. I will do a few courses in order to give myself a chance to reach my new goal.

Monday, 29 August

It is Hailey's birthday today – this time last year we were in Ardkeen, I was so deep in trouble I realised that there was probably no way out. But that this wonderful thing was happening to me anyway, and maybe it's the only reason I'm still here at all. Happy Birthday Boo Boo, I'm sorry I can't see you today. It is killing me. I know I made light of the fact yesterday but I am hurting inside. I will never forget the moment you came into the world, how I felt, how proud I was of Fiona. The last year has been bitter/sweet for me. I have a lot of regrets but you made me not give up when I was feeling like throwing in the towel. I will ring Mam soon and ask her to give you a little kiss from me … I was thinking all night about Fiona and how she has been with me over the last few weeks. She has been wonderful with everything but I still wonder if she still really loves me or is just with me for Hailey's sake or is feeling sorry for me. I wish she knew and would say so. I think I will get her to leave Hailey at home one of the days and I'll ask her to get everything off her chest. It is very fragile at the moment. If and when I go to jail I don't know if (1) she'll still be with me, or (2), if she is, if she will be able to cope on her own again. I don't know.

Thursday, 1 September

I am in my room 34 writing this, listening to Death Cab for Cutie. Not a bad album. I had my third one-to-one today, it wasn't too bad, he is starting to probe a little deeper into things. How can I expect other people to understand when I don't really understand myself how I did what I did, and how I lost everything – a good job, and thousands of euro? I am making some progress though. It is going to be a long road back to normality.

Monday, 5 September

I was working with 'R' in the Unit, checked in three more lads. It is like a conveyor belt for people with addictions, it's amazing how many people pass through the house. I found out that there were two more articles in the papers over the weekend, the same shite again, but Fiona was fairly upset about it, she was mentioned in it, and her address given. I could feel my blood boil when I heard how upset Fiona was on the phone. Fucking bastards. I don't mind them writing about me, but write only about me, and try to write near enough the truth ... Eventually I read *The Star* piece, which wasn't too bad except for the inaccuracies about the €40,000 bet in a bookies in Belfast and that I was thirty-six and from Kilkenny.

Thursday, 8 September

This is Our Lady's birthday which is a big deal in here, with visitors from all the other houses. There is a Mass this evening at 7 p.m. followed by a turkey and ham dinner at 8 p.m. I helped set up the tables for the big banquet tonight, it brought me back to my days in the Seven Oaks Hotel. Liz asked me if I would carry the statue of Our Lady, which is an honour, and I said I would do. Four of us would be in white shirts and black jeans carrying the statue around the garden of remembrance, where the Mass was being held. The weather cleared up nicely for it, and after the Mass we carried the statue. You would swear people have never seen other people in black jeans and white shirts, the amount of people who commented on it was mad. I suppose you start getting excited about anything different in here. When we were holding up the candles, singing Happy Birthday to Mary, I thought: how did I get from being Branch Manager in a post office to singing in a rehab centre after Mass and a light parade? ... A bit surreal ... The meal was lovely, all that was missing was a glass of wine. I helped clear up the tables, back into floorboy mode, maybe it was the shirt. Then there was a one-man band playing in the coffee shop. Myself and 'N' stayed for a little while before I went into the TV room and watched twenty minutes of *Lethal Weapon 4*. It was a long day.

Saturday, 10 September

In *A Million Little Pieces*, which I've been reading, James Frey described it as The Fury, and I'm feeling it today, all the old guilt, remorse, anger and resentment towards myself, embarrassment. I am a fuck-up, I don't blame anyone for hating me, I have cursed my life and all my family's lives. Sometimes I think it's all bullshit in here, I can forgive myself but I can't ever see anyone else forgiving me. It is always going to be with me. I was looking at courses in VEC but am too embarrassed to go. I couldn't wait to get on the phone to Fiona to tell her how I was feeling, which goes against everything they tell you to do in here. I was very down, I told her to sell everything, my car, camera, DVDs, CDs, and that I didn't think she really loves me anymore. That she is only with me because of the Boo Boo. I let a lot of stuff that was building up in me out in fifteen minutes on the phone, I felt like shit after, and I'm sure I made Fiona feel worse. She said she was afraid of getting hurt and of me going to jail and being left on her own. I don't blame her. I went walking in the wind and rain for an hour, didn't talk to anyone and just lay in bed thinking until two in the morning. To make things worse Liverpool lost 1–0 today, but that is the least of my worries.

Sunday, 11 September

After the family meeting (which I didn't attend, just showed them down to the assembly hall), the highlight of my day and probably my whole time here was when Fiona gave me a hug in the Garden Centre and asked me was I OK. I haven't felt so safe in a long time. My heart melted. It was like, for a few seconds everything was OK. I was on a high for the rest of the day. Went for a walk, had a good chat with the lads, came second in the table quiz and was fairly positive all night. Going into a new week, with a small bit more hope

Monday, 12 September

At breakfast one of the new men, 'A', made a beeline for me. He has been struggling for the last few days with various things and was thinking of leaving. I had a chat with him and tried to calm him down, think it worked … Was talking to Liz and Josephine about things, they were delighted to hear I was thinking of 'staying on' and eventually doing a counselling course – they told me that one of the girls that works here did a course in Kilkenny which is good for counselling. Myself and Gareth had to change the old man's diaper again – we're doing it very briskly now, with a sort of military precision. We're getting really good at it.

Tuesday, 13 September

Sr. Colette said that it was OK for me to 'stay on', so I showed her the times that me and Fiona had discussed and she was delighted with that. Sr. Colette is really happy about it, and said it is nice to see someone genuine looking to stay on. I am also very happy. Made my day.

Wednesday, 14 September

Myself and Gareth had to 'change' the old man again, but we are getting so fast at it now, it doesn't bother me as much as it did – Penance. And as for Gareth, he could never have imagined for a moment that losing his sense of smell could have an upside. It made me late for the GA meeting, but I am starting to see how the meetings work. It is nice to talk to other people who understand how and why we are compulsive gamblers, and how it takes over your life and how you can't stop. Earlier I rang Fiona, and my father and Niall, the Boo Boo is starting to feed herself. Hopefully I won't miss her first steps.

Thursday, 15 September

Just after reading a quote in the Jesuits book by Professor Emeritus Abraham Zaleznik. It really resonates with me, because it gives me renewed hope that I can come back from this.

'Leaders are "twice-born" individuals who endure major events that lead to a sense of separateness, or perhaps estrangement, from their environment. As a result, they turn inward to re-emerge with a created rather than inherited sense of identity.'

Saturday, 17 September

All the days are rolling into one, which is a good sign. It means I have structure and peace of mind, contentment, and the programme is working. After breakfast I went down to watch the Ireland v Australia game, what a result. I still run odds through my head, wondering what price each team was, but I soon rid myself of these thoughts. I suppose that's the compulsion bit of my problem, I don't know. I really enjoyed the match. I am enjoying all matches a bit more since I've given up backing money on them.

Sunday, 18 September

'M' and 'O' have just arrived in. 'O' is only back from holidays. He was off the drink for three years. He was flying to Portugal and was nervous flying. Doctor gave him Xanax, he relaxed, was delayed for two hours, started drinking. It's so easy even after sobriety for that long, all it takes is one drink. 'M' is a nice fella, very bad stammer, arrived in locked, trying to pop Valium on Friday night. A genuinely funny person. As I had a stammer when I was younger, I can feel his frustration when I am talking to him. Liverpool got hammered 4–0 by Spurs but I really don't care anymore, I am focused on other things … Fiona has won third prize in the Cuan Mhuire draw, worth €500, very ironic considering I am in here for gambling. Sr. Eileen sold her the ticket at the Family Day. A bit of good news for a change, it will pay for car insurance. I went to the AA meeting and then did the Rosary. This guy from Carlow who's just come in was actually a regular with myself and Niall in the front bar in Scraggs. I was walking past the sitting room door, I glanced to my left, and like something out of cartoon I did a double take and reversed when I saw this guy. I didn't know he had a problem but obviously he does. So I had to check him in, go through the rules with him. Just like I was, he's in the pyjamas. Later I'm leading out the Rosary at 8 o'clock in the sitting room, there's eleven fellows in pyjamas, including this guy, both of us knowing that a couple of months ago we were having pints in the front bar. I say to him, 'If only Niall Byrne could see us now.'

Wednesday, 28 September

A couple of us were asked to do a talk for a Transition Year class from Callan in Kilkenny. We went over to the Garden Centre for a coffee, then had the chat around 11 a.m. I spoke first, just gave them a brief background on myself and how and when I started gambling. I spoke a lot about the addiction and how it affects everyone around you. I didn't talk too much about the amounts involved. I found it good, and I wasn't that nervous talking. The only thing it lacked was structure. I enjoyed the meeting and the lads seemed genuinely interested in what we were saying. Another good step in my recovery.

Sunday, 2 October

My last day in Cuan Mhuire Athy as a resident. I woke up at 7, had a shower, then watched the rugby — Ireland beat Italy 36–6 and are in the quarter-finals of the World Cup. I was packed all week so I just had to throw a few things into my bag. We were all on a bit of a high because we are on our way to the last part of this, to a week in Ballycarron in Co. Tipperary. A lot of people wished us all well this morning. It is a big achievement to make it through the programme. I have learned a lot about myself and my addiction. And I can't wait to go back to Athy to do a bit of voluntary work. I am looking forward to building back up my life, it's not going to be easy, mind you. I went to meditation at 11 but left because people were talking, so I just went to the oratory and spent some time on my own. We left Athy around 1 o'clock and got down to Ballycarron around 3. We stopped at a shop on the way down. It was strange to be in a proper shop for a change.

When we arrived down I was impressed with the house and the grounds, and the Glen of Aherlow in general. The place is lovely and peaceful, but you also got the sense that this is going to be a boring few days. I feel relieved that it is all over, but I also feel a little bit sad to say goodbye to all the people I have got to know since the day I walked in the doors of Cuan Mhuire on 22 July. It seems like so long ago. There have been tough times being away from Hailey and Fiona for the past three months, I know Fiona has had a lot more. It was something I had to do because my head was gone.

I feel nervous about all that I have to face, but I also feel calm and at ease. I am a lot stronger mentally than I was when I came in, and I can't wait to get home to my family to start my new life – a second chance – the rest I will leave in the grace of God …

We walked up the mountain today … it was a symbolic event, walking up this actual mountain in the Glen of Aherlow, reflecting on the mountain of trouble which we have been facing. It was a nice walk and I enjoyed the craic with the lads.

Doing this journal has helped me in my programme and hopefully I will keep it up when I leave. So as they say in AA and GA … I'll leave it at that.

PART 4

CHAPTER 20

Not long after he completed his time in Cuan Mhuire, Tony O'Reilly lost his wallet. He was otherwise in a relaxed frame of mind that evening, at home with Fiona and Hailey, when he realised that he couldn't find his wallet anywhere.

He was seized by a feeling of panic. He really hated the idea that he might have lost his wallet, it drove him on a mad search through the only places he figured it could be, the house or the car. And his frustration deepened because after a couple of hours of searching, there was still no sign of it. Yet such was the compulsion that had come over him, he could not stop looking for it.

He describes this compulsion as being as powerful as anything he had ever felt even in the craziest moments of his gambling, and all the more crazy for the fact that all he had in the wallet was a €20 note.

This man who had lost millions was suddenly consumed with anxiety over the loss of a wallet containing €20. And he was rational enough to realise the inherent absurdity of the situation, to take a step back and try to calm down, but still the loss of that wallet was killing him – not the money, just the wallet with the money in it, a wallet of very little value in itself, a wallet of no sentimental value, except that it had belonged to him, and now it seemed to be gone.

He found it eventually, not in the house or in the car but in a van belonging to his father-in-law that was also parked outside. He was so relieved he almost cried, while still a rational voice inside him was marvelling at the ridiculous level of worry this had caused him, how the mere idea of losing just one more thing, however small, had overwhelmed him.

◆ ◆ ◆

It was the first time he had felt so vulnerable since he had finished the programme in Cuan Mhuire, although a few days after leaving it there was a reminder that he was by no means 'cured'. Again, there was only a small amount of money involved, the €50 that was handed back to him from his dealings with the shop in the treatment centre, yet he gave it to Niall Byrne straightaway to get a €50 iTunes voucher with it, as if he couldn't spend it quickly enough. And though €50 was now quite a large amount of money to him in the overall scheme, he didn't mention this transaction to Fiona. This showed that even after so long in treatment, in the harsh light of reality he was still slipping into old behaviours.

He didn't want to go into the shop himself to buy the voucher, because in these early days after Cuan Mhuire he was trying to avoid contact with the world as he had known it. He would still be going to the centre in Athy on Tuesday mornings and Wednesday nights to do voluntary work in the detox unit, but back home in Carlow in these early weeks of 'freedom' he would only go out under cover of darkness, perhaps to take Jack for a walk, generally to eliminate as much as possible the chance of some embarrassing encounter with someone who might recognise him.

He had a couple of days out with the An Post audit team, meeting two of them in the Ashdown Park, the hotel in Gorey in which he stayed when he couldn't, or wouldn't drive home from work in the snow. Two full days of full disclosure, and then it was back to his reclusive existence in Carlow.

It was a casual remark from his friend Martyn that finally convinced him he had to break out of this self-imposed isolation. He had gone to Martyn's house to pick up a few movies on DVD and as he was leaving Martyn said, 'I'll see you around sometime'.

The vagueness of it sent a chill through him, this sense that he was now existing so far outside the normal flow of life, even friends were not expecting to see him any time soon. He decided at this moment that he had to put this right. In mid-November, a World Cup qualifier in which Ireland were playing Estonia gave him the opportunity to make some kind of a return to civil society. Or at least to Scraggs, where he went to watch the match with a couple of old football pals who agreed to come down for the night.

It was good of them, and their presence helped Tony greatly to cope with the dangers of the occasion, the nostalgia for his old life that would naturally descend on him as he sat in the same snug in which he had celebrated his win on Messi and Rooney in the Champions League Final, celebrated like a man who knew that the day of judgement was near. The same snug in which Niall Byrne first started to challenge him about his state of mind, calling him 'All-In Tony' as he absentmindedly bet 'All-In' on nearly every hand, so preoccupied was he with news of the winners and losers coming through on his phone. And it turned out there was danger, too, in the fact that an old acquaintance happened to see him there in the snug, watching Ireland beating Estonia, and proceeded to talk at length about his own gambling adventures, knowing that he was talking to a man whose life had so recently been devastated by gambling, who was only emerging from a long period in treatment as a result.

Tony's head was spinning after this encounter, at the fact that he had to ask someone quietly to ask this man to stop, at the scale of the incomprehension of the addiction of gambling on the part of this person, and no doubt of many others. But he knew that he had to learn to deal with such things, that everything had changed for him now.

On 1 December 2011 he got a true sense of what that change meant when he went to Gorey garda station to be interviewed.

He felt quite calm on the way to Gorey with his solicitor, John O'Sullivan, himself a renowned figure around Carlow for his theatrical abilities, in particular his appearances in pantomimes, and the fact that he is one of the few members of his profession given to wearing a cowboy hat and a trench coat along with the more traditional suit with three Bic biros – blue, black and red – usually sticking out of his top pocket. Apart from his legal assistance, O'Sullivan was bringing something else, the fact that he was a good companion on such a journey. And all those weeks of treatment were also helping Tony to deal with this situation a lot better than he might have done six months earlier.

Yet the fact that it was Gorey, that he had travelled this road so often in better times, made it a poignant trip.

In the hall of the garda station he was arrested by Detective Ian Hayes, as he knew he would be, and cautioned. He was brought into the back office where they took his details, such as name, address, height, and marks or scars or other defining features. It was all done in a civil and laidback manner. They took his belongings, his watch and phone and belt and keys and so forth, and put them in an envelope until the time he would be released. He was then brought into an interview room where he would spend the rest of the day. It was freezing, and he kept his jacket on most of the time. He was sitting in a black chair that was fixed to the floor. It was not comfortable.

Civil and all as the proceedings were, nice and all as Detective Ian Hayes and Garda Aisling Daly were during the interview, there was something about that black chair fixed to the floor that gave him the creeps. But he drew again on his hard-won experiences in Cuan Mhuire to get him through this session, which was being recorded by a video camera in front of him, with a screen to his right that had three slots for video tapes.

Mainly they went over the statement he had made, how he started taking the money out of the €2 coin bags, and then progressed onto the notes. Tony brought the issue of his addiction into it as much as he could, as they went over all the loans he had taken out and showed him a record of his last eighteen months of betting, a frightening document.

Mainly, though, he was quite relaxed, even bored at times throughout the interview, for the simple reason that he was telling the truth. There was one thing, though, to remind him that these days, he can never be relaxed in the normal sense. John O'Sullivan had warned him that he might be locked in a cell during the break between interviews, and sure enough when they broke for lunch he was brought down and locked up and they told him they'd be letting him out in an hour.

He had been dreading this, as anyone would, and now that it was actually happening he steeled himself against it, but it was still devastating. He had known that he was hardly going to avoid spending some time in a cell somewhere for all this, and yes, he knew this would be a very mild version of what was to come. But it still gave him a powerful sense of what they mean when they talk about a shiver running down the spine. His whole body, his whole being, was shivering.

They apologised for having to put him in the cell, and he was given a burger and chips. But he was still locked up.

When the afternoon session was over, he was given back his belongings in the envelope and released on condition that he sign in to his local garda station three times a week. Christmas was just a few weeks away. He felt this was the last one he would be enjoying outside of a cell for some time.

◆ ◆ ◆

Not only did he make his 'comeback' to social life in Scraggs, crucially, thanks to Niall Byrne, he was offered a job there, starting in the new year. He would be working as a cellarman, but he was also given a couple of nights a week behind the bar. It was poignant for him to be back there, at square one. But he had been happy in this place, and it gave him this odd sense that his life was starting again. Clearly those who knew Tony well still had no doubts about his basic integrity, and accepted that the person they knew had been seized by this addiction which he was now addressing.

But those who did not know Tony well, if at all, were still going to be a natural source of anxiety. He was still quite paranoid as he walked the streets – often he would pretend to be on the phone – but when he started working behind the bar in Scraggs there would be no such escape.

He recalls a post-Christmas party of people from a large store in Carlow, who simply couldn't stop staring at him. While he was in the front bar, they would come in from the back bar, and he would see them pointing at him. 'There's your man.'

The job was giving him back some sense of self-esteem, though, a sense of structure in his life that was further enhanced by his voluntary work with the new arrivals into the detox unit at Cuan Mhuire. He dealt mainly with those in for gambling.

And every day he would have to deal, too, with his own crisis, trying to make amends to the family whose lives had been irrevocably changed by his addiction, trying to face up to what was yet to come. Trying to deal with situations he had never remotely imagined himself being even associated with, such as his next trip to Gorey in March 2012, to the district court to face the charges, which at this point numbered twenty-four in all.

Setting out from Carlow at 8.30 a.m. with John O'Sullivan, he was determined to be upbeat, or at least to seem that way for Fiona. He was also sustained by the support he had received in Cuan Mhuire, both in the house and at the GA meetings. On arrival in Gorey garda station he was met by Detective Ian Hayes, who had arrested him for the first time in his life, and was now arresting him for the second time. He was processed and then the charges were read out to him, all twenty-four counts.

He was trying to stay calm, but he was getting more nervous as the time approached when they would have to leave for court. A car was sent up to check for the presence of the media, hopefully to avoid them as much as possible. He was told they would be walking, which was disturbing to him because it meant they would have to walk past the post office. As they passed the scene of the crime, they encountered none of Tony's former workmates, though he did see one female colleague going out to breakfast. Mercifully, she did not see him.

Tony, John O'Sullivan and Detective Hayes went into the café opposite the post office, with Tony still feeling this surreal sense of embarrassment at the thought of his former colleagues coming in and seeing him. The garda, the solicitor and the defendant had coffee, with Tony finding himself in the same seat in which he had entertained the An Post auditors that Christmas. Then it was into the courthouse, which was crowded at 10.30 a.m., though to Tony's relief he could see no one waiting outside for him, no reporters or photographers.

In the courtroom he could see Niall Byrne and Tony O'Reilly Senior, who had come to support him. Tony Junior observed the procession of cases, the drink driving offences, a few small robberies, even in one case the robbery of a set of rosary beads. He felt that he didn't belong here, and yet the fact of the matter was that he did.

Just before lunch he was called in front of Judge William Early. He was granted bail of €1,000, he would surrender his passport and sign on every Saturday at Carlow garda station between nine in the morning and nine at night. He was granted legal aid and told to come back on 3 May to receive the Book of Evidence. He felt it was all fair enough for such a serious offence.

There were reporters in the room, and Niall Byrne would tell Tony that they seemed to be 'going hammer and tongs' when he was in front of the judge. On the way out he saw a photographer, though his first impression was that he was looking for pictures of a man who was in court that day on charges relating to a fatal hit-and-run at the crossroads up from the post office. Tony remembered the incident well from when he was working there, in that other life which was now so far behind him.

Then Tony realised that the photographer was taking pictures of him and John O'Sullivan, though oddly enough he seemed to be concentrating more on John, as always wearing the cowboy hat and the trench coat. It seemed funny at the time, but it was not funny at all a few days later when the *Carlow Nationalist* and the *Carlow People* splashed the story all across the front pages, with pictures and full reports on the imminent downfall of this prominent member of the community, the 'post office boss'.

Of the many horrible experiences Tony endured in these dark times, his exposure to the tender mercies of the media was among the most dispiriting. But then the mood swings that were constantly assailing him could be triggered by anything, at any time – like the night in Scraggs when someone, as a 'joke', presented him with a cake on top of which stood a miniature version of himself dressed in a striped prison uniform and carrying a ball and chain, handcuffed to a prison officer.

It wasn't even his birthday, it was someone else's fortieth, but they knew he would be coming in with a group of people to mark a big occasion of his own. That occasion was the end of a six-month foundation counselling course he had been doing for two nights a week in Butler House, in Kilkenny.

He had seen the ad on Facebook for this course, which cost €1,500 and, as it happened, he had received a tax rebate of €1,400. Although they were enduring serious financial hardship, Fiona had agreed that for Tony to do the course would be the best possible use of the money in the long term. They were determined that some good would come out of all this, that his future was in counselling and that if he was serious about it, he had to do this certificate course. Which he did, and which indeed would turn out be the right thing to do.

At the end of the course he was having a meal in Lennon's restaurant in Carlow with eight other people who had done it with him, and then they moved the celebrations on to Scraggs, where this birthday gathering was taking place. And there, astonishingly, he was presented with the cake with the 'jailbird' on top of it – which must have seemed to someone like a kind of going-away gesture. Usually he could see the funny side of these things, but this time he was finding it hard. He wouldn't eat any of the cake, or agree to have his picture taken with it. But he tried to stay in control, marking it down as just another sad misunderstanding of where he had been, and what he was going through.

In May he received the Book of Evidence – his case was clearly serious enough to be sent forward to the Circuit Court. On some days he could steel himself for the prospect that he would almost certainly be going to jail, but sometimes it was all too much. Like the day his solicitor told him of a case involving a fifty-one-year-old man who had robbed €250,000 for gambling purposes, and who got three years. Or the first meeting with his barrister, the junior counsel Colman Cody, who banished any illusions that all the 'positives' might keep him out of jail – the positives being the success of his rehabilitation so far, his voluntary work in Cuan Mhuire and the counselling course. All of which were commendable, of course, but the barrister felt it would still not be enough to spare him a sentence, which he was now advised might be four years.

On the good days he had been hoping for two years. When he left that room with his notional sentence doubled, he found that he couldn't hold back the tears, they seemed to be streaming down his face involuntarily as he walked away from the meeting with the barrister, past the Carlow post office, to his car – the same post office where it had all started for him, as a part-time postman, so long ago it seemed.

On 6 July, as he prepared to plead guilty to six counts of theft and six counts of changing documentation in front of Judge Barry Hickson at Wexford Circuit Court, his senior counsel, Patrick McCarthy, was even more uncompromising than his barrister had been. He grilled him before the proceedings as the prosecution barrister would be expected to do, in

particular on the need to show that he had indeed gambled all the money. The Gardaí, aided in no small way by that jaw-dropping record of every transaction that Paddy Power had eventually released, would ultimately decide to accept that Tony had indeed lost every cent of it. That even his extravagances, such as they were, consisted of gifts to betting shop employees after a big win, a habit that endeared him so much to the staff of the Gorey branch of Paddy Power that one of the women working behind the counter knitted a cardigan for Hailey. At the Carlow branch, on his birthday they had given him a Liverpool FC jacket and a jersey.

Judge Hickson ruled that he was to return to Wexford for sentencing on 16 October. So that was the day he would find out what his fate was to be. His father and Niall Byrne were in court, but he knew that the day was coming when they would be leaving the building without him. And if he needed any more proof that his life had shifted permanently into some other weird dimension, as he left the court Tony used a fire escape to get away from a press photographer who was sprinting after him.

The man who had started out as a part-time postman was now dodging the paparazzi.

CHAPTER 21

On the morning of 18 December 2012, Tony O'Reilly packs his bag. If the gods had selected the saddest time of all for a man with a baby daughter to be preparing to go to jail, they would probably have gone for this time, this very day even, one week before Christmas.

It couldn't be otherwise. His sentencing hearing in October had been postponed until today, but there could be no more postponements or adjournments. This was it, the day he would be given a sentence for theft and fraud. For Tony, there could be no more imagining that he might not go to jail – though even at this stage Fiona was still hoping that somehow he would come back home tonight.

He was receiving so many good wishes from so many people, it might have seemed that the moral force of that alone could defeat the brutal realities of the law. He had been giving talks in schools, representing Cuan Mhuire, a mark of how they regarded the progress he had made in his recovery. He wanted that association to continue. It was already becoming clear that he would make an excellent counsellor in the area of gambling addiction – indeed, given the astronomical scale of his own gambling, the fact that he had somehow come out the other side of it would place him among the world's leading authorities in the field.

What good could possibly be served now by putting this man in jail, when he would clearly be of far more benefit to society on the outside?

Fiona and his friends and family who were still clinging to the hope of a suspended sentence did have common sense on their side. The night before this decisive court appearance he'd had three pints of Heineken with Niall in Scraggs. Niall still believed that a strong argument could be made for a non-custodial sentence. Tony tried to convince him that the law was against it, the numbers involved were colossal, that he would be going down. He'd reassured Niall that whatever happened, he would be all right, that all the work he had been doing would enable him to cope.

Earlier that day he had stopped to get petrol in the garage on the Tullow Road, and as he looked across the road he could see a Paddy Power office. It was a strange sensation, another of these moments of incomprehension that it had come to this. That one day, a long time ago, he had walked into a Paddy Power office, and here he was now, packing his bag for jail.

It was a hard bag to pack.

John O'Sullivan calls for him at 11.00 a.m. He says his goodbyes to Fiona and to Hailey, who has been sick for a few days and who was not in great form anyway. There is the slight possibility that this will not be goodbye at all, but the odds are long. Tony would not have backed himself to win this one, not with bad money, as they say.

He is wearing a grey suit that he had bought in Dunnes Stores the previous week for €100. He hates wearing suits. As usual with John O'Sullivan, the journey is interesting, and some of the driving could be described as unusual, but they arrive at Wexford courthouse shortly after 12.30 p.m. There they meet Sr. Susan of Cuan Mhuire, who has agreed to speak on his behalf. Liam and Ellen of the Cuan Mhuire staff have also come to support him.

The photographers and reporters have come too, and for this one the television cameras as well. Wexford Courthouse is a modern building, which enables the photographers to get right up to the door of the courtroom. But at this early stage of the proceedings they hold fire – the case will not be heard until later in the afternoon. Tony will not be meeting his barristers until after 2.00 p.m., so he and John O'Sullivan and the party from Cuan Mhuire head for lunch in The Vine restaurant. Tony has fish and chips and salad, which he is pretty sure will be his last meal as a free man. Everything has this heightened dimension now, every fear is coming to pass, it is all closing in on him. His last day, his last meal, his last moments before being led away to the prison, which he has accepted as his fate.

Fiona, his mother and father, Niall Byrne and two old friends from Cuan Mhuire, Richie and John, arrive at 2.00 p.m., and then there are the meetings with the barristers, Patrick McCarthy and Colman Cody, during which it is made clear again that the best they can hope for is a reduced sentence, that they will concentrate on how well he has progressed in his rehabilitation. Indeed, he has already figured out that the only way he can get through a jail sentence will be by observing the ancient advice of the fellowships, to take it one day at a time. Now the photographers are hard at work, and he is aware of them taking pictures even when he is on his way into the toilet.

At 4.40 p.m. Judge Pauline Codd starts to hear evidence from Detective Ian Hayes. As Tony sits in the main body of the courtroom beside John O'Sullivan, not yet formally separated from his fellow man, he hears Detective Hayes speaking in a humane and generally helpful way, describing how Tony had risen so fast in An Post he had been known as the golden child, accepting that all the money had indeed been gambled and used for no other purpose, but making an impact on all sides when he mentions the number 'ten million' which had been staked overall, including a bet of €40,000 on the Norwegian ladies football team.

This became the hook that would feature in so many reports, the bet that would appear so crazy to the general public, which had not been properly informed that every day of the week thousands of men all over the world are betting on propositions as crazy as that, and in fact considerably crazier than that.

Sr. Susan then stands up to describe, in layman's terms, the mind of the gambling addict, how it differs from that of, say, the alcoholic, which might be likened to a washing machine with its different speeds, the fact that it slows down sometimes and then speeds up. Whereas the mind of a compulsive gambler is more like a spin-drier, going all the time at high speed. She speaks so highly of Tony and the work he's been doing in Cuan Mhuire, Tony has to wipe away the tears, listening to such kind words, reflecting on all the damage he has inflicted. He has already supplied the judge with an eighteen-page statement of everything he has done and the remorse he feels, the story of his life and how it has gone so wildly wrong.

Shortly after 5.00 p.m. Judge Codd remands him in custody for sentencing the following day. Now he knows for sure that he will be going to jail, it is just a matter of how many years. He stole €1.75 million from his employer, and he is going to have to pay for that. Fiona is crying and the others are in a state of shock as the prison officer comes over to put on the handcuffs. They are called figure-of-eights, these handcuffs, which to Tony feel so indescribably strange, rendering him unable to move his arms. He is led from the court and out to the back gates, to where the prison van is waiting, the dog-box as it is known.

It is dark now. As he makes that long walk to the van, keeping his head down, he is conscious of the flashing of the cameras following him all the way.

◆ ◆ ◆

The journey in the prison van takes about three hours. They have to go to Shelton Abbey, near Arklow, and then to Wheatfield with another prisoner, and then he is brought to the Remand Centre in Cloverhill prison in west Dublin. For a while he is in a filthy cell which, by some cruel arrangement of the gods, has 'Gorey' etched on the wall. Then he is processed and given prison clothes – a grey tracksuit with a green polo-shirt, a vest, underwear and socks. He is put into a holding cell with a chap called Eamon, who is due to be sentenced for assault and battery. They get on quite well, indeed Eamon has heard of Tony's case. They are led to their cell for the night, which has two bunk-beds, a TV, a kettle, a couple of half-litres of milk, tea bags, sugar and cornflakes.

The toilet is in the corner of the room, and is open. After chatting with Eamon, he settles into bed without a pillow, and falls into a deep sleep. He wakes suddenly, nearly jumping out of bed. This continues all through the night, falling into what feels like a deep sleep, then waking up with a sense of panic.

When morning comes he is given back his clothes, then placed in the holding cell once more to wait for the journey back to Wexford in the dog-box. He is handcuffed again, even when he says he is starving and they stop at a petrol station on the way down to get him a toasted cheese sandwich and a bottle of water. It had never occurred to him how difficult it might be, trying to eat and drink while handcuffed.

Arriving at Wexford courthouse, he has to wait in the van for a while. He can hear someone asking the prison officer which way they'll be going in, so the RTÉ camera and the rest of the photographers can get what they want.

When he gets out of the van, handcuffed to the officer, he knows what to expect. But if anything, the officer is more unnerved by the cameras and the reporters, which would be comical, except in his anxiety he is more aggressive than he might otherwise be, adding to the impression that Tony is being dragged into the courthouse – 'like a dog', as one of his friends describes it. These wretched images would be seen on the RTÉ News that night.

At 11.30 a.m. by the red digital clock, Judge Pauline Codd starts to speak. From his new position in the accused's gallery at the side of the court, Tony listens to her outlining his fate. He starts to feel strangely calm, almost detached from the proceedings, as if having an out-of-body experience. In Cuan Mhuire they had advised him to say the 'Memorare' prayer during these moments, and it seems to be working.

'Remember Oh most gracious Virgin Mary, that never was it known, that anyone who fled to thy protection, implored thy help, or sought thine intercession, was left unaided. Inspired by this confidence, I fly unto thee, oh Virgin of Virgins my mother; to thee do I come, before thee I stand, sinful and sorrowful. Oh Mother of the Word incarnate, despise not my petitions, but in thy mercy hear and answer me, Amen.'

He keeps saying it to himself over and over. The simple rhythm of the words seems to be working as a sort of anaesthetic.

Another bit of advice he got from someone in treatment in Cuan Mhuire was that if the judge starts talking about the positive stuff first, you're in trouble. It means the bad stuff will be coming at the business end, as it were.

This judge is talking about the bad stuff first – the breach of trust, the enormous amount of money, the fact that Tony didn't seek help before he hit rock bottom. And then she moves on to the better stuff – his full co-operation with the Gardaí, his recovery, the fact that he is hard-working and charismatic.

He hears the judge saying the number 'six', which startles him for a few moments. He looks at Niall, who is concentrating intensely on the judge; he sees that Fiona's head is bowed. But he hasn't been given six years. He realises that the judge is going through the options, that 'six' isn't the final verdict.

The judge finally reaches the sentence that he must serve: four years, with the last one suspended. This will probably work out at about two years in real time. It is at the lower end of what he had been expecting, and though friends and family are still upset at the verdict, for Tony, who has thought of little else for a long time, this is about as good as he'd ever imagined it.

The ordeal of the day is not yet over. John O'Sullivan had been unavoidably absent due to another case, and he rushes in at the end, angry that it has gone ahead without him, given that he has been involved all the way, both as a solicitor and a family friend. There is nothing John can do to change the course of events, however. Tony is going to jail.

Now there is some talk about getting him out of the court through the fire escape, to avoid another session with the media. As these negotiations go on, Tony stands on his own to the side, powerless in so many ways. He is hoping for this one small thing, that they'll take him out some quiet way, unseen by the reporters. But a garda shuts down this modest vision of compassion, declaring that justice must be seen to be done.

Once more Tony is taken out through the front door, 'like a dog', to the van. He will have to wait for a couple of hours for another case to conclude. Finally, they get underway, bound for Wheatfield Prison in Dublin. As the van crosses Wexford Bridge, there is a small part of the window through which Tony can see the lights of the town that they are leaving. His eyes are full of tears.

'Thank fuck', he is thinking. 'Thank fuck this is over'.

CHAPTER 22

From the journal of Tony O'Reilly, prisoner 83719, Midlands Prison, Portlaoise.

It is Saturday, 29 December and it's the first time I've written a journal since I arrived in the Midlands. After one night in Wheatfield I was transferred down to Portlaoise early the following morning, again I had to get back into my grey suit. I will definitely fuck that out as soon as I can.

That first night in Wheatfield in Clondalkin as prisoner 83719, which I will be for the next three years, I was trying to be calm but my thoughts were mainly with Hailey. That, I think, is the hardest part of everything, and will be for the duration of my stay in jail.

The check-in procedure had been just about as horrible as I expected it to be. I arrived at a counter with a holding cell to the left, containing a number of fellows who were jeering and shouting at me – 'what are you in for?' – not because of anything to do with me, I don't think, just jeering at anything really. At the check-in they take note of tattoos and other identifying marks, which gave me this strange sense of being some kind of an animal having the brand checked on the way to the slaughter.

Then it got very weird when it turned out that the next officer checking me in was someone I knew from playing football, making it an awkward situation for both of us. We just kind of nodded at one another as he gave me a small towel with carbolic soap, part of a 'welcome pack' containing a toothbrush and toothpaste, a pen and some paper. Then he directed me to a booth where you get changed out of your clothes, leaving you with just the small towel which you hold around you as you sit on the X-ray machine, which examines you for any contraband you might have hidden about your person.

I had none, so I went on into the shower cubicle. Next I changed into my prison clothes, a kind of a tracksuit, and was brought up to the landing, a quiet landing it seemed – but maybe it just felt that way because I was still getting over the jeering of the lads in the holding cell. Still I could sense an atmosphere of tension and a kind of menace. There were pool tables in the middle of the hallway, and from my days working in pubs I always associate the pool tables with trouble, for the simple reason that a lot of trouble tends to happen around them. I guess that nervousness is heightened another few notches when the pool tables are in Wheatfield Prison. It was just before 'banging out' time in the evening as I was put into my cell.

This was it, my own prison cell. I was finding it hard to focus on any one thing so I was hopping from writing my journal to reading to watching TV. In fact, I was able to watch myself on TV. There I was on the Nine O'Clock News, being dragged into court and dragged out of court and into the van. It was a completely surreal experience, sitting there in the cell in Wheatfield looking at my own story being covered for about a minute-and-a-half, hardly even recognising myself with the bloated stressed-out face, and that Dunnes Stores suit. I'm thinking, 'Jesus, that can't be me.'

The news programme also had stories about Christmas and how people are coming home for Christmas. It was breaking my heart. I had to turn it off.

I feel so ashamed and guilty about everything, it's going to be hard to stay strong through all of this. Things are never quite as bad as they seem but in this case I don't know. This is going to take all the 'tools' from the tool box Cuan Mhuire gave me. I am waiting for the meltdown, hurting inside, really hurting.

One good positive on the day I was sentenced is that justice was finally done for the ninety-six victims of Hillsborough, RIP. So I will remember 19 December for two contrasting reasons. And I am sure as I go forward there will be more positives and hopefully some of my fears will not be as bad as first thought.

Arriving down to Portlaoise from Wheatfield the next morning, I spent most of the day in a holding cell and arrived up at my new 'home' in C2 at about six. It was a long enough day but I got fed rice and bolognese and a pint of milk, which kept me going.

I was met by a familiar face, 'Mike' from Carlow, who is helping me to settle in. Mike is maybe a couple of years older than me, a well-known criminal as they say, although I mainly remember him as a lollipop man. I now realise he may have been doing some community service at the time.

Otherwise I knew him only from serving him in the post office, but he's read all about me in the papers, and despite his reputation, it's a really good thing he's doing, because he's come out of lockdown to help me out here, walking with me on the landing.

Lockdown means you're in your cell for twenty-three hours, it's your own choice. And since Mike has been in jail for about twelve of the last thirteen years, it's a choice that must be very important to him. So Mike is putting himself out for me in a big way, and I feel that this is a great stroke of luck.

He even got me some clothes which were better than the jeans which were too big for me, and the maroon shirt and jumper. They were thrown in the bin. I also got a pack with two vests, two white y-fronts, carbolic soap and shower gel, a shit toothbrush and toothpaste. I was put into cell 32, a double cell which was clean and OK. I was on the top bunk with a shitty foam mattress, a telly and a kettle. In fairness, it could have been a lot worse. I stayed up pretty late settling in and watching TV with my new room-mate, Seamus from Drogheda, who's in here for arson – he set fire to his partner's house.

The following morning I had a lie-in because I was shattered after the previous two days. I had to go down to see the doctor, who didn't understand addiction and was very dismissive about my story. I asked to see an addiction counsellor. Dinner was next at 12, and then back to the cell to eat it, lock down until about half one-two o'clock, then the landing open until about four. Then tea, lock down till half-five. Two hours on the landing until half-seven. Then lock down for the night.

I have a shower every night at 7 p.m., in one of the communal showers on the landing, which is something I was dreading before coming in here, just from watching all the frightening stuff that happens in prison showers in the movies. But it's been safe enough so far, maybe thanks to the power of Mike. There's so much lime in the water though, he advises me to shower under a J-cloth, and I think he actually means to put one directly on your head, which I can't really bring myself to do, lime or no lime. It means that every day in here is a bad hair day. You can't drink the water either.

So I had a routine fairly early on. For the first few days I spent a lot of time in the cell, with a good few visits. But generally kept to myself and asked a lot of questions to familiarise myself with the ins and outs of prison life.

My Da dropped in a few phone numbers and photos of Hailey which I got that night. I have been trying to block out all sad feelings about people on the outside. One of the lads said that it is the brain's way of coping, and not to feel guilty. I try to block them out, but I'm not really succeeding. At any time of the day I can be hit by a wave of pain or regret for the life that I threw away, with all its softness, bringing me here to this hard place in which even the most ordinary thing can suddenly give you a rush of fear.

I started in the Officer's Mess on Sunday, which was pretty soon after I arrived. Hopefully that won't go against me with other prisoners. If it does, I guess I'm in serious trouble and there's nothing I can do about it. The food is so much better here. The days are long but it means that I am off the landing, which is good. Two of the lads off C2 are working there as well, we are getting on very well.

The remainder are from A wing, which is where they're keeping the sex offenders, the 'jockeys' as they're called in here. They are totally segregated for their own safety, and only a certain type of prisoner – I suppose the likes of me who is not regarded as a 'career criminal' – is allowed to associate with them in situations like this, working in the Mess.

Fiona and Niall came in on Christmas Eve, but no Hailey. I was filled in on everything on the outside, and got a good visit because I work in the Mess. Some of the lads in Carlow chipped in so that I could buy a PlayStation 2, but I will probably hold off until I get a single cell, maybe not. It could be a distraction as I have a lot of reading and writing to do. I am slowly cutting out all the crap, white bread, etc., and hope to start in the gym tomorrow. I also plan to go out to the yard for some fresh air as I have not been outside in over ten days. But I am doing the right thing by taking my time and not rushing into anything and settling in properly.

I have written a few letters and will write more when the new year comes. I received a nice letter which Fiona dropped in to me from a person who went through something similar in 1996. He has since gone to college and is an addiction counsellor with the Pathways Project in Dublin. It was nice to get a letter from a random stranger and I wrote back outlining my plans, which are also in the direction of counselling. I also wrote to Sr. Susan, Ellen and Chris, Joe and Mag.

Regret, shame, guilt, loneliness come in waves, but I keep myself busy and am trying to stay focused on all my plans and goals. My mind is relatively clear, my skin is clearing up after the stress of everything.

I was told something that stuck in my mind. That you are in jail, so act like a criminal. Which I take to mean that I shouldn't be thinking of myself as some kind of a special case, who only did one big crime and will probably never do anything else of that nature. They say the other prisoners can sense it off you, if you think you're not like them, or are putting yourself above them, even subconsciously. And they don't like that.

Tuesday, 1 January 2013 8.30 pm

It is New Year's Day and I am writing this while listening to Dave Fanning in my new single cell (No. 4). I was moved in here yesterday evening and while it is a filthy cell, it is good to be in on my own. It is also easier to write here, as I can rest assured that it is locked during the day when I am in the Mess. It has been a mixed few days.

On Sunday morning I read an article in the *Sunday Independent* by Declan Lynch about me, which was very positive. I wrote back to him today to thank him for his different point of view. It really had me on a high for the day and I phoned a few people to make sure that they saw it.

I have some stuff arriving from reception tomorrow as well, which will make this experience a little more bearable, namely my music. I will be seeing Hailey for the first time tomorrow, which makes me a bit nervous, how it will go.

I was back in work at 7 on Monday morning, but that was OK as I was excited about seeing Hailey later in the day. Niall, Fiona and Hailey arrived at 11 o'clock and I had to hold the tears back when I had Hailey in my arms. She clung on to me for fifteen to twenty minutes. I could see the love in her eyes, and that she had missed me.

They told me that there is a lot of goodwill and support out there for me, which is good to know. I managed to hold everything together for the visit and after about an hour it was time for them to go as Hailey was cranky/tired. I went back to work with a drawing Hailey had done, something to remind me of things that are now so distant to me, things like innocence and beauty.

When I came back to the landing I spent the evening moving into my new cell. Then I was locked down for the night. I had a sad night in general, a lot of things going through my head. I tried to sleep early but couldn't, so I got back up and wrote a letter to Declan Lynch and then rang in the new year looking at RTÉ coverage with Imelda May, amidst the deafening noise of hundreds of inmates banging down their cell doors.

On the television I have this view of the outside world, with people celebrating and letting go of their troubles for a few hours at least, while I am here, cut off from all that, in this mad world full of rage, of men 'celebrating' the new year by making as much noise as they can, noise that nobody outside this hellhole can hear. It was quite surreal really, something I won't forget.

Wednesday, 2 January, 8.15 pm

I am sitting in my cell listening to Pearl Jam – 'Black'. Over the last hour I have had a mini-disco of 80s indie songs with a bit of Muse thrown in. I got a few things from reception today, my music being the most important. It is all about the small things in life. A few CDs and a Sony Walkman has made my day. It gives you a certain freedom for a few minutes or even a few hours, to let you forget where you are, and for how long more you have to be here …

Pearl Jam – 'Breath' – what a tune.

Days here are grinding away, moments of sadness, of anger at what I let myself become, but also I am trying to allow myself moments of hope about the future. It could be a lot worse, and believe me it is a lot better with some music.

People say in here that you come in alone and you will leave alone, which is so true. One of the lads that I was getting on with from C2 and the kitchen was not in work this morning. I later heard that he was moved to a different prison because he was a dead man walking. I heard a commotion on the landing last night but thought nothing of it. But this morning I heard that a load of lads from the upper landing had threatened to get to him.

It is amazing how quickly things can change. It really made me see things a lot more clearly – don't get too pally with anyone and keep the head down at least till I get to an open prison.

A dead man walking – that's what they said. I had been chatting to a dead man walking, someone who was in great danger of being actually murdered, the kind of thing I had only seen on TV. Maybe unbeknownst to myself I was preparing my head for this when I used to be watching episodes of *Prison Break* with one eye while keeping the other eye on the road to work in Gorey.

I heard yesterday that the house opposite us in Sandhills was a grow house for cannabis and was raided the other day. Gardaí, fire brigades, ambulances everywhere. I suppose it will take the heat off me for a bit. There was nothing in the *Carlow People* about me this week, which is good.

Got new blinds for my cell today – nice bits of cardboard. The joys of jail. As I said, it's all about the small things.

Friday, 4 January

I have decided to try to do one positive thing here each day – mainly for myself, or to make my time here a bit easier. Today I asked about getting my wedding ring back and sorted out who I would get to do my laundry for a half-ounce of tobacco or 'dust'. Hee-hee, the stupid fucking names of things in here. Doing your 'whack' (your time), 'parking it offside' (hiding something or someone), and being 'wide' (knowing things) are just some. I am here two-and-a-half weeks now, and no one is going to tap me on the shoulder and tell me it's all been a terrible mistake, that I can walk out of here. So I'd better learn the language and a few other things.

And Mike, who I'm starting to notice has a vague resemblance to Ian Brown of the Stone Roses, is always there to fill me in on the finer points of prison life, like bringing me a load of posters to put up on the walls – he even brought the Blu Tack for them. He came into the cell and told me I couldn't have no posters on the wall, everyone else has them. The others might think there was something wrong with me if I didn't conform by having these Page 3 pictures and this poster of Kelly Brook that he brought in. So they're up on the walls now, along with a big one of Al Pacino as 'Scarface', and one full of quotes by the Dalai Lama, just to balance things out a bit.

I am also reading a book about writing [*Writing Alone and With Others*] which is pretty good. Because I'm thinking that some day this story of mine might end up as a book, which is another of the positive things I am trying to do, and will hopefully continue to do.

What good thing can come out of this horror-show? Well I suppose if my story ever got written down, it might do some good, for someone. It probably wouldn't do me any harm either, to get it all out. Maybe if I'd read a story about a guy who'd had a nice life and who ended up in a place like this through gambling, I might have got out of the game a bit sooner.

So I'm reading this book about writing, and the main things I'm getting from it are not to rush writing, and to write without fear. Two things I have been doing a lot of the time while journalling.

So here it goes – I don't know if I will ever write a book about my life, but I think I will have a stab at it. I have a story to tell and I have to do it my way, and for the right reasons, if only for Hailey to be able to read it and to realise what really happened.

Sitting here drinking tea, *A Question of Sport* on the telly in the background, facing a terrible green wall that is still filthy after the last person here. Metal door to my left, metal bars to the window on my right. A wire mesh for a window. Books stacked before me to my immediate left – *1984, I Know This Much Is True, Shantaram, The Prisoner of Heaven* – my green tray with my plastic fork, knife, spoons and teacup to my right, tea bags and sugar. But above me are pictures of Hailey and me, a card with a picture of a beach on it. Memories of happy times gone by, and still to come. My cell floor needs to be painted and a few posters to brighten up the walls, then it is home sweet home for a while.

I look forward to getting some decent writing paper and pens, it's all about the small things. Maybe the school will have them. That will be my positive thing for Monday, to see Ms Fogarty who is over the schools. My haircut is Sunday, so it's all go-go-go …

Other than that the majority of the A wing lads in the Mess are fucking children who are only working there for food to sell for drugs – but hey, it's not like I will be hanging around with them on the outside, so I grin and bear it.

Sunday, 6 January

Writing while listening to Muse – *Absolution*.

How do I feel today? I woke up thinking, 'fuck me, I am in jail'. There's these few seconds just before you wake up properly when you're not fully conscious of your surroundings, and part of you is not aware that you're still in a cell in Portlaoise. And then you're fully awake and it hits you again and you have to face the truth all over again – that you're here for another day, for as long as it takes. It was an up and down day, but I definitely need something to tax my brain, so I sent home an order for some of my books on addiction and counselling. If I could do an Open University course in counselling here, I would.

Tuesday, 8 January

A guilty pleasure – I am sitting here in No. 4 listening, sorry, bopping away to 'Blue Savannah' by Erasure while writing this. A bit of a change from Muse. I have had a pretty good two days and am on a kind of a high. I think your head starts to make adjustments in here, so that things you wouldn't even notice in the real world, like being able to listen to music, start to seem precious. It's a way of coping with the basic madness of it all, I'm sure. Today I was organising the 'school', I have applied for social studies, music and creative writing, so hopefully I will start one or two of them shortly. There is also a good chance of getting to do an Open University course. You have to have at least honours English, luckily I have a B. I knew it might come in handy one day. Even in work everyone is starting to get along a lot better, which makes the day go quicker. But one negative, today and every day – I really miss Hailey and her little ways and I can't wait to see her on Thursday. I may order Milky Way for her tomorrow …

Thursday, 10 January

Being in here is sometimes similar to being in Cuan Mhuire. While you are trying your best to get on with things, and make the best of a bad situation, it's the time frame of visits and phone calls from the outside that can fuck you up in the head. You have two six-minute calls every evening, to five or six designated numbers that you contact by dialling one to six. But if you go straight through to voicemail, you lose the call. Or if the call drops for some other reason, you've lost it. And if you do make the call from start to finish, that six minutes or hour can make or break your day or your week.

Today I had a visit from Niall and my Dad, Fiona and Hailey. Without realising it, Hailey breaks my heart every time I see her. All she wanted today was not to be there, and it killed me. It's not her fault, she is only two, but it still hurts.

I think Fiona is only going to bring her over every second week from now on, and only wants me to ring every second night. How is all this going to pan out? Fiona deserves to be happy, and she won't get that with me …

But my Dad told me something of note today, that he reckons there's some kind of a TR [*Transfer*] organised for me in the coming weeks. I find that very hard to believe, unless it is for a section 42 [*Further Questioning*].

On a lighter note, I finally got my hair cut for a half-ounce of 'dust' from this other prisoner called Declan, so I still did my positive thing for the day, and I got my laundry organised. So just the PlayStation to organise now and I am fully settled in, hee-hee. Hopefully school will start soon or, better still, I'll get to do that Open University course. I need something to work on, to keep me sane. In fact maybe there's none of my sanity left to keep, but I just haven't realised it yet.

Friday, 11 January

Friday night in Cell 4 listening to 'Stairway to Heaven', rocking it out. It's a bit sad how I always put the music I'm playing in my journalling but hey, fuck it, it's my journal. I had a shit day in the Mess. I am working with two dickheads. Children and complete assholes. It's hard not to say something, so I have decided to bite the fuck out of my lip. The Mess is the quickest way out of jail or into an open prison, so I am not going to jeopardise anything by saying something to these lads from A wing.

Hopefully a few more lads from the C2 landing will come up to work there. Anyhow I am not going to let them affect my days, just keep the head down. And I also have to stay focused and not let the outside world affect me 'doing my whack', it's bad enough dealing with the negativity in here.

I built a little bookshelf out of cardboard today to organise my books. On Monday I am going to start my getting-fit regime so I can have a clearer head for study.

Saturday, 12 January

Went to Mass this morning and did a reading. The sister called me after and asked me my name and complimented me on my reading. It was nice to be appreciated. The more people I get to know in here and how I interact with them, the better the chances I have of an open prison sooner. It's also nice to have some prayer time to reflect on things. I am a bit tired, and changed my mattress around and got a second pillow, so hopefully I will start to get better sleeps. I will be easily pleased when I'm back on the outside. I will be able to bring everything back to basics and lead a simple life … we will see!

Sunday, 13 January

It's Sunday night and I am wrecked and my neck is killing me. Some craic in the Mess, one of the lads took the laser out of the CD player so the A wingers couldn't hear their stupid dance shit and of course I got the blame. But I don't care. You could cut the atmosphere with a knife. Fucking idiots.

Hopefully school will start this week and I have a few more visits to look forward to, so the week should be OK. Got my new TV with a remote supplied by Mike, another small luxury.

Mike is trying to pump me for information about post offices systems, so he might be able to rob the money without getting caught, but I just tell him to fuck off, and really we both know that nothing will come of this. It's like he's trying to make out that he's only helping me because he thinks he can get something out of me. When the truth is he's actually doing this out of the goodness of his heart. But you can't admit that kind of thing in here.

I am giving him something back though. Because I work in the Mess I don't eat at the same time as others, so I bring my dinner back to the cell. I give him my dessert.

There is another lad starting in the Mess tomorrow so it should ease the work load and he is from our wing which makes it that bit better. Man U beat Liverpool 2–1, I will ring my Da tomorrow to ask about that possible transfer and to ask about that letter I sent to Declan Lynch. He will probably publish it as he must be stuck for things to write about, cause he wrote about Alex Ferguson today. Boring!

Listening to PJ Harvey … not bad.

Monday, 14 January

'You may get to the point where you realise that if you want happiness, you have to accept profoundly and honestly the sadness that waits at every turn. Every decision for happiness will get you in trouble, and your occasional courageous forays into the dark will likely give you a taste of heaven. Opposites weave back and forth into each other, like a thousand yins and yangs inter-penetrating…'

Thomas Moore, *Dark Nights of the Soul*

Thursday, 18 January

I deserve to be here but don't belong here. That thought ran through my head a few times today. This place is exactly what I thought it would be – full of anger, full of indifference. People pulling against the system just for the sake of it. No remorse, just plans for the next big scheme. Full of who's bigger and who's who.

I stay away from all that bravado and just want to get out in one piece without being sucked into anyone else's way of distorted thinking. It can so easily happen. It's all about wheeling and dealing in here, all of them trying to be the top dog. The one who can get things. You give me an ounce of tobacco, I'll give you sleepers [*sleeping tablets*] for a week.

You have €15 credit or 'grat' in the shop, but the real currency in prison is the 'dust'. And usually by Tuesday evening everyone is nearly out of dust and people are constantly in arrears with payments and that's all you can hear all evening as prisoners go from cell to cell in search of a fix. In fact I give my half-ounce of Amber Leaf tobacco to Mike at that time, and he can charge double for it.

I don't use it myself. The only time I've really felt like smoking was during that RTÉ New Year programme, it must have been causing me a lot of stress.

I was actually out earlier while bringing out the bins, and sucked in as much fresh air as I could. I saw the wall that I noticed when I arrived here nearly a month ago, and as it goes it will probably be the last of the Midlands Prison I will see when I am leaving.

I got to talk to Hailey briefly, she didn't want to come on to the phone, so I had to coax her onto it. But she is doing well which is the important thing.

I got a letter from Declan Lynch today which was great to read and could be the start of a friendship … and he could be a good help if I ever do write a book. He states that coming through addiction is like having two lives, before and after, which is a bonus other people don't receive. Maybe that is why I was always sorry, and accepted what was coming, because I was at the start of my new life. A life without gambling.

My release date is 18/03/15. Time to try and chip away at that.

21 January

As I sit here writing, the landing is a hive of activity. Everyone scurrying around trying to get dust or tablets to make their nights go quicker, easier, or in a haze.

There was a better atmosphere in the Mess earlier, and as far as I know there are two new lads from A wing starting tomorrow which will keep me out of the wash-up area altogether.

Today was probably my best day in here. I started school which was very good, I did creative writing today, and it was only myself and the teacher Geoff in there. It went very well and we chatted non-stop for the full two hours. We talked about *The Shawshank Redemption* and the imagery, and how it's better to show than tell in essay and short story writing. We read a passage from a book and I found myself talking and talking. It was like I really needed to talk to someone other than a visitor or a phone call or a fellow prisoner. I just had to offload on someone.

It was also great to talk to Hailey again today when I rang my Mam and Dad. I love the way she says, 'hi Daddy' and I can't wait to see her on Thursday. While I think of it, I may bring paper and a pen to keep her occupied. All in all a good start to the week with a tinge of sadness while I think about Hailey. Xx

22 January

It's nice to get a bit of good news every so often when you are 'on the inside'. I rang John O'Sullivan this evening. He is coming over on Friday to discuss a possible early transfer. I won't get my hopes up too much about anything that involves an open prison TR or any community service, but it is still nice to hear that it may be a possibility. Hope is what it is all about, hope!

I am going to try to get the counselling workshop finished by the weekend, just something I'm doing for myself, from a tape. I really want to do everything I can to be a counsellor and to turn this horrible experience into something good, that's the plan. I have a load of reading, writing to do. Slow down, there is no rush. There is no rush. There is no rush.

23 January

I got a nice card from the girls in Bon Appetit [a delicatessen across from Scraggs] today. It's nice to think that random strangers take the time to write. It's a bit overwhelming really and fills me with hope. The way I deal with things in here is to break it down into segments. Hopefully 6–8 months for an open prison, then hopefully 6–8 months for Transfer after that. Then maybe Athy, then home.

Mike tells me that when he was in lockdown, as a way of keeping sane he read the whole of the Bible and learned all the words in the dictionary, from A to Z.

I'm not going to be here for that long, but I do wish this was all over, I really do. Bang! The door closes for another night but this is the time I enjoy. Time to read, time to write, while all hell breaks loose outside. Shouting and roaring. It is their way of making the day interesting, I suppose. Thank God that I am off the landing all day, I would go mad if I had to listen to that shite.

I had some pretty weird dreams last night. That I had done the fraud all over again, for 4 million this time, and was trying to explain my way out of it. I felt so hopeless and scared and feared another 5–10 years in jail, but I woke up relieved it was only once I did it. Relieved that I was only serving three years.

They are making a decision tonight about whether C wing is to move over to the new building. It will be obviously be much better than this one, in the sense that the facilities in the cells will be much better, but still I hope this doesn't happen because the single cell makes life easier.

25 January

Click. Click, the door re-opens at 6.30 a.m., not the full lock, just the electronic one. I know the time and know that I have a little more time to sleep. I had a good night's sleep and was still tired by the time I got up at 8.15 a.m. That's the thing about working in the Mess, you are fairly tired by the time you get back to the landing – physically and emotionally.

It can be a quick day and a long day all in one. As I sit and write this, all I can hear is murmured rumblings of convicts and the phrase, 'bang it out'. I have already done this, as I do nearly every evening. It gives you some small sense of control being able to lock your own door rather than having it locked for you, but once you've 'banged it out', it stays locked till morning.

The boxing is the main thing to get them started. You hear two lads starting to box one another while everyone eggs them on … Something to talk about for the next two days … I always miss the fight because it is nearly always left until half-seven for some reason. It is now quiet, everyone locked up for the night, click, bang. There goes my door until the morning.

I need to talk to someone about my whole home situation. It is clear to me now that myself and Fiona have grown apart and I want her to get on with her life, but how do I say it's all over? By letter? In a visit? I think she deserves a bit more than that. Maybe there is no easy way to do it. I want Hailey to be happy and I am not happy and won't be until I get all this sorted out. I need to talk to Emma the psychologist and will try to organise that along with the school next week. Maybe I am putting too much pressure on myself. Maybe I can talk to Niall about some aspects of it. Another week nearly over.

26 January

I am getting huge feelings of guilt about what I have put people through, especially Fiona. She didn't sign up for the shit I landed her in. She has stood by me throughout the court case and the time leading up to it and has dealt with a lot of stuff. None of it her doing. But in truth the problems probably go a lot deeper and I don't think my long-term happiness lies with her. All I want is for her to be happy too, I think she deserves that much, and she will never be truly happy with me.

Working in the Mess I look after the preparation of the salads and while making coleslaw, Ace of Base's 'All that She Wants' came on the radio and it brought me right back to Fat Bob's diner in Portlaoise, and the video jukebox, twenty-one years ago when I was seventeen. In the kitchen there, making tubs of coleslaw, listening to the music of the time. Little did I know that a lifetime later I would be doing the same in a totally different set of circumstances.

How can I resolve the real issues in my life, my marriage, while locked up? Please, someone give me the answer. My head is spinning, spinning, spinning, just like the days of my heavy gambling.

4 February

I was told that I was rejected for Shelton Abbey, but it was passed later. I don't know what this means, maybe I will be gone in a month. It will be sooner rather than later, I think. Today I finally see what real jail is like. The tension on the landing was unbelievable. It's half-six and someone is going to get butchered, I am told. For the next hour about ten lads walk up and down the landing side by side, eyes bulging, looking for the right time to strike, everyone armed with horrible home-made weapons — toothbrushes with blades burned into them, or just pens that they can stab you with. Everyone gathers at their doors, a crowd gathers at the bottom of the landing, the intended target and his cronies.

It's all political and playground stuff, but with far more serious consequences. It's the first time that I really feel alien to this place. It is nerve-wracking, but for once I stay at my door to see what happens.

It's more than just curiosity on my part, there's a mad animal energy out there, and in some small part of you, deep down, you are getting drawn into it like the crowd at a big boxing match waiting for the bell for the first round. At bang-out time nothing had happened, but it will probably happen tomorrow. I don't know, but I do know it's pretty intense stuff, frightening really, a world so far removed from the one I am used to – I don't belong here, yet I deserve to be here.

My kit went missing with bedclothes and a few bits and pieces. The only thing I will miss if it doesn't show up is my Nike tracksuit. Everything else is pretty shit. It is more of an inconvenience really. It was mainly my whites for work.

Hailey says she can't wait to see me on Thursday – me too. X

5 February

Wednesday evening sitting watching England v Brazil. I saw my first signs of a row in C3 last night. Some travellers boxing with nails between their fingers. Loads of blood. Also the Cork lads had their turn of walking up and down the landing in this show of strength. I doubt that is the end of it. It will probably kick off one of these nights. Pretty scary shit all the same.

My clothes showed up after being missing for a day. Brazil have just equalised, just as England were bigging themselves up as world beaters again. Champions League back next week – cool. My Mam, Niall, Fiona and most importantly Hailey coming tomorrow.

England back in front – world beaters again.

7 February

It is now Friday evening and I am relaxed after a day away from the mess. Niall, my Mam, and Fiona were in yesterday and the visit went

OK. Hailey was in good form and it was great to see her. Nice to see my Mam too, for the first time in here. It was tough, though, when Hailey wanted to go. She gets bored, she can't help it. She is having trouble going to the toilet but Fiona brought her back to the nurse. It went OK, I was worried that she had a twisted bowel or something.

Liam from Cuan Mhuire came today and it was great to talk to him and offload a lot of what was on my mind. He told me to come up with a plan of action for a couple of things, so I can rebuild my life. It's not going to be easy, but not impossible either.

PATIENCE, PATIENCE, PATIENCE.

I am in Room 16 in Shelton Abbey and everything is so much better. Last Monday week in Portlaoise, during a visit, an officer came in and said I had to wrap up the visit ASAP. I thought someone was dead, the way he came in.

I was shocked and excited when he told me I was going to an open prison. Someone is definitely looking down on me. My luck seems to be changing at last.

It was all a bit unnerving, and I was in a kind of a frenzy when I was packing up my stuff. Prisoners in and out of my cell making smart comments, looking for posters, bed clothes, anything they could get their hands on. I was glad to get out of there.

Mike came into the cell, and I thanked him for his help and support. I had four or five half-ounces of tobacco left, and I gave them to him. We said we might see one another when we got out, and left it at that.

For someone wanting to be a counsellor, I had learned how wrong it is to be judgemental, how someone like Mike might be regarded by the normal world as nothing more than a criminal, yet he had shown himself to be capable of such generosity. Certainly I owed him a lot more than the few bits of tobacco I was able to give him.

I made my way down to Reception, weighed down with all my stuff. Declan – the one who cut my hair – was also on his way to Shelton Abbey. After about two hours, during which there was a slight suggestion that we might have to wait till the next day, we were on our way in the dog-box – handcuffed.

Odd that we were handcuffed on the way to an open place where you can just walk out. On the way the tears flowed with relief and joy that I was going to somewhere I can fit in a bit better. My time in the Midlands had come to an end.

But I had learned a lot, especially about myself.

We arrived fairly late to Shelton, a fine old building just outside Arklow, and got checked in – my fourth jail, but it was not like any of the others.

We were even shown the best way to leave. This place is based on trust, which will suit me down to the ground. I was put into a six-man room and was on the top bunk, but I didn't care. This place is like another world. Phone calls when you want, using call credit. Doors that are not locked. The ability to go for walks around the grounds when you want, and so much more – iPods, food brought in, more clothes, proper visits, even ducks wandering around outside. It is amazing really, after where I've been.

It gives me the opportunity to get fit, to learn to do my whack in the best possible way. I will be here for a good chunk of my sentence. The lads in the room were sound, and I settled in very well. The bed was uncomfortable but I didn't care. I have since moved to a different room (16), a four-bed which is a lot better. I have a locker and wardrobe here. I have my DVD player, iPod, and loads of books. I have really enjoyed the freedom of phone calls. I have called everyone on my list.

Hailey came in with Fiona and my Da on Sunday and seeing her in a good environment was brilliant. I will keep my head down and hope my time goes quickly. I can't get over the difference in the two places. The hardest part here is to keep the mind busy, which will suit me. The whole thing is to keep to yourself and stay out of some of the shite that goes on here.

I got a job in the Officers' Mess, which is handy enough, and I will be able to do a bit in the school as well. I have put in for history and creative writing, and I hope to be able to work on my own book in time, because Jesus I have some story to tell.

I have started to walk and to exercise a lot, so it's all about patience, and doing the right things so that I can firstly get weekends out, and then out for good as soon as possible.

It is going to be hard but I think the worst is behind me, and I am really looking forward to a new life. I am as happy as I can be, in my present circumstances.

CHAPTER 23

The sentence was thirty-six months in total. The best that Tony O'Reilly could possibly hope for, availing of all the options available in the prison system, was to get out under the programme of Community Return in eighteen months. That is exactly what he did.

Rather than 'languishing' in jail, he had decided that the only way to make it bearable was to use it as wisely as he could, to make it the start of something, not the end of everything. And then to get the hell out of there as soon as he could.

He had done that foundation year in counselling at the PCI College in Kilkenny, and now he enquired about the follow-on course, a Bachelor of Science in Counselling and Psychotherapy. In reply to his query he got a letter saying that the course was still open, but there were two problems: first, he was in prison; and then there was the €4,250 per year he would have to pay this year, and for two years to come.

Though he was told by one or two otherwise sympathetic people that he surely wouldn't be able to manage that, he did in fact manage it. Somehow, with money gathered from family and friends, from a charitable organisation and even from a leading clergyman, who responded to his letter with a cheque for €1,000, asking only that this not be made public, he was able to pay for the course for the year, and eventually for the two years after that. This involved making use of the rehabilitative programmes of the prison system to the extent that he was freed every Tuesday from Shelton Abbey, collected in Arklow by a friend, and brought to and from Kilkenny for the day's education.

He even got the limited use of a mobile phone, a pink one, oddly enough, as part of a new policy that was being tried in the prison for low-security inmates. And he joined in anything that might give him some sense of well-being, like the 10k run around the grounds of Shelton that was organised through the prison school, as a result of which Tony and other inmates each made a few hundred euro for the Our Lady's Children's Hospital, Crumlin. The run took place on 30 May 2014, the day of his fortieth birthday.

That evening he was re-reading a book called *Zen and the Art of Happiness*, by Chris Prentiss, which had been dropped into him during his early days in the Midlands Prison by a good friend who had supported him then, and would continue to do so after he left Shelton. He found a quote in it that had helped him through the tough early days in prison and the darkest days since. He would eventually get it tattooed on his lower right arm.

What good thing will come of this?

For the last six months of his sentence he was allowed out on Thursdays to do voluntary work at Teach Mhuire in Gardiner Street in Dublin, using a voucher to get the bus from Arklow to the city. Teach Mhuire is a transition house for those who have been in the treatment centre in Athy, a 'clean' house where they can stay for a few months to get their lives together. And though Tony might have been of more use there developing his counselling skills, he was happy enough sweeping floors, just to be away from jail for a few hours.

Even though Shelton is an open prison, it is still a prison, and even an inmate as determined as Tony O'Reilly to make the best of it will have some terribly dark days. One of these was the day he left Shelton to visit his mother, Colette, who was recovering in hospital in Waterford from an operation for breast cancer. Their relationship had been strained by the pressures of Tony's case, but it had not always been so. He remembers mostly good things during his teenage years and through college, but he also remembers – indeed it will stay with him to his last day on Earth – that look of disappointment on her face when he came back from Carrickfergus. It was as if the €8,000 he had 'borrowed' from her had turned it all into a kind of a personal betrayal, making the hurt that bit harder for her to bear.

As he left Shelton to get the bus to Dublin, and then from Dublin to Waterford, he was hoping that something might change for the better between them, that he might at least be able to shake off this feeling that he had been partly to blame for her illness by bringing all this trouble into her life. There was really no way of knowing this, but he worried about it anyway.

To get to the General Hospital he had to get another bus in Waterford, and since he also had to get 'home' that night to Shelton, it turned out that the round trip left him with little more than twenty minutes with his mother. That would not nearly be enough, in the circumstances. In fact, if anything he felt worse after the meeting, which brought back to him a lot of feelings of guilt and shame, eating away at him on the long, long journey 'home'.

But there was a day worse than this. It was the Sunday when Hailey became unsettled as she was leaving with Tony's parents after a visit. She grabbed on to Tony's neck, crying uncontrollably, as the others tried to separate them. When they had prised her away, she grabbed on to Tony's legs with the same determination. She knew he wouldn't be going home with them, and it seemed to trigger this primal reaction. Tony, in his own way, was inconsolable.

There is a school of thought that an 'open' prison is a relatively pleasant environment – relative at least to that of a high-security prison – and this is true up to a point. But those who make such a bland assertion would perhaps need to witness such scenes before they make a definitive judgement.

This moment with a distraught Hailey was the hardest thing he had to face in prison, harder than the humiliation of the check-in procedures, harder than being on the landings in Portlaoise, harder than the thoughts of all that time still to be done. He was advised later by a counsellor that he had to imagine that soon after they left through those white gates, in all likelihood Hailey was playing with her toys in the back of the car, engrossed in something else.

Whether this was true or not, there wasn't much that Tony could do about it, where he was.

Nor could he prevent the *Sunday World* running a story on him getting out of Shelton to go to Kilkenny for the day, a large two-page feature that left the viewer in no doubt that the *Sunday World* does not view these 'progressive' measures in a positive light.

'Exclusive … We Pay for Jailed 1.7 Million Gambler … To Help Addicts' was the headline under a picture of Tony on the bottom left-hand side of the front page, directing us to a two-page spread inside. 'Bet To Society' it proclaimed, above a piece illustrated with three pictures of Tony – getting out of the white prison van carrying his rucksack, standing on the side of the road in Arklow waiting for his lift to Kilkenny, and talking to the *Sunday World* reporter.

He had been approached by the reporter and, after identifying himself, he stated that he had no comment to make. Clearly she had been tipped off that this was his routine. It was a brief encounter, during which a photographer sitting in a car nearby took the pictures of Tony that accompanied the piece, which started like this: 'A chronic gambler who went on a multi-million betting spree with stolen post office savings is training to be an addiction counsellor on a taxpayer-subsidised course' [in fact he was paying for the course himself].

It went on:

> Our pictures show 'Tony Ten' O'Reilly free as a bird – despite being sentenced to four years behind bars less than a year ago.
>
> Here he can be seen being dropped off by a prison van at the main Dublin road in Arklow – his own personal taxi service. The former compulsive gambler enjoys the fine weather while waiting for a lift to Kilkenny from a friend. When approached by the *Sunday World* the dad of one said he couldn't comment about whether he thought it was fair that he was out and about …

The theme of Tony's supposedly cushy lifestyle, 'free as a bird' and 'enjoying the fine weather' and so on, was revisited in a picture of Shelton Abbey with the caption: Privileges.

They probably missed a trick too, when you consider that the infamous murderer Malcolm MacArthur had left Shelton shortly before Tony's arrival, and that Tony was now doing the job MacArthur used to do, cleaning up after lunch and hoovering and generally tidying up the officers' mess. He was told that MacArthur had been 'very prim and proper', and that on duty in the mess he was given to wearing a white coat of the old-fashioned type that grocers used to wear.

The *Sunday World* might also have mentioned that Tony's destination on the day they confronted him, Butler House, where the PCI College is based, is itself a very fine old building, a most agreeable establishment in which to spend time – but yes, Shelton Abbey is a truly exceptional house, the former seat of the Earls of Wicklow, 'lavishly embellished with reducing buttresses with tall pinnacles', and beautifully situated beside the Avoca river.

It doesn't feel quite so palatial, though, when you're Prisoner 83719.

◆ ◆ ◆

Tony O'Reilly was released from Shelton Abbey on 24 June 2014, eighteen months after the judge had sentenced him to a three-year term. The euphoria of that moment was flattened somewhat by the fact that there was still some time to be served on the outside. This took the form of 'Community Work', which involved picking up litter around Carlow three days a week, or cutting grass, trimming hedges and weeding footpaths on the New Oak housing estate.

As Tony says, you would learn humility pretty quickly out there.

He also had to sign in once a day in the garda station, and once a week in Portlaoise prison. Although the people overseeing this probation period were generally the decent type, it was clear to Tony that there would be no great transformation in his life just because he had got out of jail. There was no neat formula whereby you did your time and then it's over and you can forget all about it, and everyone else forgets about it too.

His marriage to Fiona was not transformed, it had clearly come to an end. There was nothing for it now but the draining procedures of separation and eventually divorce, and whatever arrangements needed to be made to ensure that he could still have a relationship with Hailey – this was the thing that really mattered to him now.

Again, there is no formula here, no law of nature which states that when a person emerges from addiction, those who have been affected by it are able to emerge from whatever they were going through, and everything resumes in a much sunnier atmosphere. While it can happen, and in the movies it usually does happen, sometimes it doesn't happen, and this was one of those times.

Likewise, Tony would find that nothing would be the same again in most of his encounters with the world he used to know, that a prison record and the notoriety that comes with it make so many routine activities just a bit more complicated. But he had sensed this anyway. He had realised from his earliest days in jail that there was just one job now for which he was supremely qualified, and that was in counselling others so that they mightn't end up in the same region of hell in which he had lived – or if they did, to show them that there might be a way out of it.

And then, his mother was dying. She had gone into remission from the breast cancer, but it had come back. The day he had been released from Shelton to visit her in hospital had not gone well, but when he got out in June, he hoped to rebuild his relationship with her.

He did not have much time to make amends. Not enough time, as it turned out. Colette would live for just five months after he was released.

When it looked as if the end was coming, the various family members went in to have their last moments with her. When it came to Tony's turn, he apologised to her one last time and told her that he was determined that one day she would be proud of him.

She told him that it was all right, that she forgave him.

Then she added this, her last words to him: 'It was very big though, wasn't it?'

Five months wasn't near long enough, but he was very glad that he got to have that time with her, and that he got to say goodbye. He never got to say goodbye to Mike, his ally and protector in prison, who died without warning in a tragic accident in which he sustained a stab wound to the leg. He bled to death in the family home. It was mainly a case of bad luck. He was forty-six years old.

It was mentioned at Mike's funeral that despite the fact that he had 'gone down the wrong road', he could be a generous sort. But they weren't aware of one particular act of generosity, the way that he had made Tony O'Reilly's time in the Midlands prison a lot more bearable than it might otherwise have been.

Such are the people you may meet when you go down the wrong road.

CHAPTER 24

On 16 August 2016 an event was held in Cuan Mhuire in Athy to celebrate fifty years of the institution, which had been founded by the legendary Sr. Consilio. She was there on the day, along with invited guests such as Miriam O'Callaghan and Fr. Peter McVerry and Minister Frances Fitzgerald. Among the speakers was Tony O'Reilly, who had entered the building at the lowest point of his life in July 2011, and who had recovered sufficiently to become an addiction counsellor there, and to be able to deliver a twenty-five-minute talk to a crowd of 300 people about his personal experience.

There was a kind of banquet in a marquee in the grounds, then it was time for the various speakers. Tony had been asked to do this by Liam McLoughlin of Cuan Mhuire, who was aware that he had spoken in schools many times during the last few years, and that he was very good at it. He was able to speak with wisdom and passion about the addiction of gambling in general, and as for his own story, at the mention of the number 'ten million', he would usually have their full attention. Liam McLoughlin had also seen Tony's progression from his arrival as a resident, to his initial role in Athy, working in the drugs detox unit, to the full-time position in Gardiner Street as an addiction counsellor, a facilitator at aftercare meetings or in one-to-one sessions, working with people who were trying to reorganise their lives, to find themselves again.

Liam knew that Tony could do this, and Tony knew he could do it too. Despite his nerves as he surveyed the size and the eminence of the gathering, he knew that he would be able to keep going somehow with his speech, because he felt there was somebody else listening, who wasn't there. As he stood up there telling his story, he found something that he didn't expect to find. He found this connection with his mother, and he felt – no, he was sure – that on this day, she was proud of him.

◆ ◆ ◆

Tony has been finding himself again, too. He is divorced from Fiona, but he sees Hailey frequently, usually at weekends in Waterford where he is based; the rest of the time he is in Dublin, staying overnight in Teach Mhuire. He is in a relationship, living with his new partner in Waterford. He is still on the best of terms with Niall Byrne, their friendship if anything deepened by it all. He sees his father frequently, grateful for his endless loyalty and for his advice on so many thing they never thought they would encounter. He is extraordinarily busy, and will no doubt continue to be, as the gambling epidemic continues to claim its victims. He hasn't had a bet since that Saturday in Carrickfergus in the summer of 2011, and he has no desire to have a bet – at least not today, as they say in the fellowships.

His life is as difficult or as easy as the life of any man struggling to keep body and soul together in the modern world. He is still paying back credit union and bank loans. But he has no addiction to maintain. He is on the other side of it now.

◆ ◆ ◆

This is the thing that strikes him, on the day he is sitting in the office of Cuan Mhuire in Athy, a newly qualified counsellor waiting for his first client. He is on the other side again, where he can contribute something, where he can do something constructive, rather than the side he had known for so long, where he was the one with the desperate need – the need to escape the boredom which he now realises must have been eating away at his soul, the need for the excitement of betting and the illusion of winning, the need for the money to keep betting, these needs that could never be satisfied. And then the need for understanding, for advice, for the truth, the need for help. In a few minutes someone is going to come through that door with all those needs, and now he, Tony O'Reilly, will be on the other side. Now there will be someone who needs him.

That person will not be fully aware that the man on the other side of this deal is at this moment probably as nervous as himself. He will not be aware that he is going to be Tony's first client, he has enough to be worrying him, of that there is no doubt.

But Tony has all the qualifications, both of the formal kind, the kind marked by certificates and diplomas, and of the kind that can't be measured by any marking system or by any other sensible means. The kind that can only be achieved by going through it all, by knowing what it is like to destroy yourself, and then to embark on the recovery of self, in rooms just like this, in situations like this, with people like this.

It is a small room, a 'box room'. There is no table in the room, just a chair for the counsellor and a chair for the client. The chairs are comfortable but not in any way luxurious, the kind you might see in the foyer of a modest hotel. The appointment is for 2.00 p.m. Tony is there at 1.40 p.m., reading the notes, trying to form a picture of the man he is going to see, trying to stay calm.

He knows how this is supposed to work. He is not there to give a lecture, but to listen, and to guide the client in the right direction. This person may well be feeling what Tony himself was feeling on that day he first checked into Cuan Mhuire. Indeed, the room in which he is now sitting, Room 11, is right beside the door of the detox unit, which he had entered a few weeks after it all went down in Carrickfergus, shattered in a thousand ways but relieved, too, that something had ended, and something else was starting.

There is a picture on the wall, a snowy scene painted by a former resident. Tony studies it, letting his mind drift down the years, remembering all the winning and the losing, that first bet on Holland, those last days on the run across the border, the magical double on Bobby Zamora and CSKA Moscow that paid €5,000 for a stake of €50, the bet he needed to win to pay for his wedding in Cyprus, the time he wanted to quit while he was ahead but got sucked into the Galway races, the night John Terry slipped and hit the post in the penalty shoot-out, the time he danced with the dog on his shoulders in the kitchen because he had got half a million back, the madness of losing most of it the next day, the day he was a guest of the Paddy Power corporation at the Curragh, knowing that in a few days it was going to be all over, all the times that someone hit the bar when they should have scored, all the last-minute goals that had broken his heart on that long and treacherous road from one euro to ten million euro … the night that Hailey was born, and he sat in the waiting room of the hospital in Waterford, looking out at the lights of the car park, knowing he was going to lose this happiness, that he was going to lose everything.

Short of dying, he could not have paid more heavily for his addiction. His marriage was over, he had lost the good job he had, he had become notorious. He had served time in jail, things that had seemed totally unimaginable to him had become his everyday fare. But then to be sitting here, in this situation, had also been unimaginable to him on the day he arrived at Cuan Mhuire.

He remembers his own vulnerability on that day, which makes him feel determined that this should be a good experience for whomever is going to come through that door. Then again, it was wrong to assume anything. Maybe this guy just wanted to waste a few weeks in here to get his relations off his case or to swing a reduced sentence.

Whoever he is, there is a procedure he will have to follow, with his counsellor, Tony, running through a formal statement about issues such as disclosure and the guarantee of confidentiality.

It is nearly time now.

It feels to Tony O'Reilly that at 2.00 p.m. he will not just be starting a new career, he will be starting a second life. He has always felt he might be good at something, he just didn't know what it was. Now he feels a quiet surge of joy as he realises that this … this is it.

And now it is time.

The man who walks into Room 11 is roughly the same age Tony was when it all started to get away from him. As they introduce themselves, Tony is taking in just the superficial things – the fact that this man is from Waterford, that he has a beard. He will find out more soon enough. Tony reads him the formal statement and then he asks the man what has brought him here.

'I have a gambling problem …'

ACKNOWLEDGEMENTS

In John Banville's *The Book of Evidence*, the main character Freddie Montgomery states that 'I do not seek my Lord to excuse my actions, only to explain them.' I felt the same when agreeing to work on this book with Declan. I am not trying to excuse my actions in any way, and from the beginning I took full responsibility for what I had done. It was a very tough decision to make, to write about my experience with a gambling addiction, as I am very aware that it will open up old wounds for some. When reliving the experience in narrating it for Declan, I became even more aware of the effect it must have had on some people.

I know that my actions affected not only my family and friends, but former work colleagues, management and the wider community. I would like to take this opportunity to sincerely apologise for any distress I caused people, especially in An Post. It was never my intention to hurt anyone, but I am sure my actions had a profound and negative effect on many. I was in a position of trust and I let a lot of people down who had invested a lot of faith and effort in my professional development. For this I will always feel regret.

However, I have managed to get back on my feet, and honestly I couldn't have done it without the support of many people and organisations. There were plenty of dark times when I wanted to give up, but the good will of some amazing people kept me going. I would like to give thanks to the people associated with Cuan Mhuire, especially Liam who has journeyed with me throughout this life-changing experience. To my family who have helped me so much over the last seven years or so, and continue to do so. To all my friends, especially Niall who has stood shoulder to shoulder with me throughout this. To the people of Carlow who have been so genuine, understanding and supportive. There are a couple of people that I didn't mention in the book for various reasons, but I wouldn't have got through this without them. Simply, thank you.

I would like to thank Declan and Gill Books for their understanding, patience and help in allowing me to tell my story. It has been a long and sometimes challenging process, and from the start Declan has been extremely supportive. I feel that I not only got the perfect person to write my story, but a friend for life. I would also like to thank my partner for her unwavering support throughout the last two years. This book would never have been written without that support.

I always said I wanted to get my side of the story out there, to show how easily this could happen to anyone. Hopefully it will help to highlight the dangers of problem gambling, a huge issue in Ireland and getting bigger by the week.

My mother's last words to me were, 'I forgive you, it was big though, wasn't it?' This book is dedicated to her memory, as she didn't get to see my journey back from the brink. I am donating my portion of the proceeds from the book to ÉIST Cancer Support Centre in Carlow, who helped her so much in her final weeks, and to Cuan Mhuire, which in essence saved my life and gave me fresh hope for a new beginning.

Finally, to my daughter who has been my inspiration to pick myself back up and to start living life again. You are the reason I kept going, and I hope when finally you hear about my story, you will understand and see me for who I am, and not my actions in the past.

I have never been happier, it is just a pity I had to go to hell and back to get here.

Tony O'Reilly

RESOURCES

If you or someone you know is struggling with a gambling addiction, here are some organisations that may be able to help.

Problem Gambling Ireland

Working to prevent and minimise gambling-related harm in Ireland. Its aim is to provide some independent supports and resources to anyone whose life has been negatively impacted by problem gambling.

Website: www.problemgambling.ie
Email: info@problemgambling.ie
Phone: 089 2415401

Gamblers Anonymous

Gamblers Anonymous (GA) is a fellowship of men and women who share their experience, strength and hope with each other that they may solve their common problem and help others to recover from a gambling problem.

Website: www.gamblersanonymous.ie
Email: info@gamblersanonymous.ie
Phone: 01 8721133 (Dublin), 087 2859552 (Cork),
086 3494450 (Galway), 085 7831045 (Tipperary),
087 4266633 (Kerry), 087 1850294 (Waterford).

Gamble Aware

Ireland's national organisation devoted to increasing awareness, improving education and funding treatment for problem gambling.

Website: www.gambleaware.ie
Email: info@gambleaware.ie
Phone: 1800 753 753

Dunlewey Addiction Service

Support, advice, training and counselling for anyone affected by addiction.

Website: www.dunlewey.net
Email: admin@dunlewey.net
Phone: 08000 886 725 (NI), 1800 936 725 (ROI)

Cuan Mhuire

Cuan Mhuire is Ireland's largest voluntary provider of addiction treatment services and residential rehabilitation. Its main objective is the rehabilitation of persons suffering from alcohol, drug and gambling addictions.

Website: www.cuanmhuire.ie

Phone: 091 797102 (Galway), 059 86 31090 (Kildare),
063 90555 (Limerick), 021 7335994 (Cork),
028 30849010 (Down)

Rutland Centre

Helping people transform their lives by providing the highest quality of research-based treatment and aftercare services in addiction.

Website: www.rutlandcentre.ie

Phone: 01 4946358

Email: info@rutlandcentre.ie

Samaritans

A confidential 24-hour service providing emotional support for people who are struggling to cope, including those who have had thoughts of suicide.

Website: www.samaritans.org

Email: jo@samaritans.org

Phone: 116 123 (UK), 116 123 (ROI)

Note: Asked to comment on the case of Tony O'Reilly, a spokesperson for Paddy Power provided the following statement:

We don't discuss the details of individual customer accounts, past or present, but we are continually evolving our responsible gambling procedures and improving our interaction with customers who display signs of harm. There are, naturally, positive developments in our approach now from the time of this case.